HOW TO
INSTALL A NEW
DIESEL ENGINE

PETER CUMBERLIDGE

S

SHERIDAN HOUSE

This edition published 2006
by Sheridan House Inc.
145 Palisade Street
Dobbs Ferry, NY 10522
www.sheridanhouse.com

First published in Great Britain by
Adlard Coles Nautical in 1993
Second edition published by
Adlard Coles Nautical 2006

Library of Congress Cataloging-in-Publication Data

Cumberlidge, Peter.
How to install a new diesel engine / Peter
Cumberlidge. – 2nd ed.
p. cm.
"First published in Great Britain by Adlard Coles
Nautical in 1993 ; Second edition published by Adlard
Coles Nautical 2006."
Includes index.
ISBN 1-57409-224-3 (alk. paper)
1. Marine diesel motors-Maintenance and repair. I.
Title.

VM771.C86 2006
623.87'236—dc22

2006016006

ISBN-10: 1-57409-224-3
ISBN-13: 978-1-57409-224-0

Printed in Great Britain

Contents

    Electrical bonding ❖ Propeller shaft anodes ❖ Cooling
    jacket anodes

8   SEA TRIALS   86
    Fuel ❖ Engine oils ❖ Gearbox oil ❖ Engine coolant ❖
    Sterntube greaser ❖ Starting up ❖ Under way ❖
    Maximum revs ❖ Continual checks

9   USING A POWER TAKE-OFF (PTO)   92
    Engine manufacturers' PTO kits ❖ Belt tension

10 PTO AUXILIARY EQUIPMENT   99
    Engine-driven fridge compressors ❖ Bilge and deck
    wash pumps ❖ Hydraulic power

11 HOT-WATER SYSTEMS   116
    Fitting a hot-water system using a calorifier

12 HOT-AIR HEATING FROM THE ENGINE   122

13 FITTING A PROP CUTTER   125
    The Spurs cutter ❖ Mounting the cutters ❖ Mounting
    the wedge holding block ❖ Prevention of electrolysis ❖
    The stripper prop cutter ❖ Circular blade cutters

    ADDRESSES OF MANUFACTURERS AND SUPPLIERS   133

    INDEX   138

Preface

The first edition of this book developed from my own experiences when we installed *Stormalong*'s present engine in 1990. *Stormalong* is a fairly heavy-displacement gaff cutter, built in 1936 of fine Scandinavian redwood and hard English oak. Her 6-ton hull is easily driven but really needed a new engine between about 24 hp and 30 hp. When we embarked on this project I soon discovered a whole fascinating area of engineering knowledge and tricks of the trade of which I'd hitherto been largely unaware. This short book is really a distillation of what I learnt in the process and my intention has been to pass on this information for the benefit of others who decide either to install a new engine themselves or oversee a new installation carried out by an engineer.

Actually choosing a new engine turned out to be a more complex task than I had imagined, partly because we were fitting a relatively compact 'new generation' diesel into a space once occupied by a physically much larger and completely different shaped petrol engine of venerable vintage. At the time, within the feasible power range for *Stormalong*'s hull, I picked out 11 engines as possible contenders, all of which had different pros and cons in terms of size, weight, performance, ease of installation and maintenance, and of course cost. From this original list I finally decided on the Perkins Perama M30, a three-cylinder 30 hp diesel in what was then Perkins' new compact range of marine engines. The Perama turned out to be an excellent choice and has served us well, and was also by far the best value engine in our original comparison list.

However, the Perama no longer exists as a Perkins model. Not long after our engine was installed, Perkins and Volvo Penta entered into an arrangement whereby Perkins ceased to market engines under 80 hp themselves and instead supplied base engines for Volvo Penta. Since then, developments in engine technology have continued steadily and now, in 2006, there is a different and even better line up of marine diesels in the 24–30 hp range. Yet though we now have improved engines and components to choose from, the important principles of sound installation haven't changed. A sophisticated new marine diesel will give long and reliable service only if the whole installation is well engineered and thought out, and it is to facilitate this process that I have produced this new edition of *How to Install a New Diesel Engine*.

1 | Choosing a new engine

The time had finally come. *Stormalong*'s elderly engine, which had helped us out of many a tricky spot over the years, was starting to become temperamental. I'd never minded a little moodiness once in a while, so long as it *was* once in a while. I could also understand a certain wheezy lethargy on particularly chilly mornings – it's no joke, after all, to be kicked into action at dawn after a cold night at sea.

But there had been some recent 'incidents' that, although perhaps forgivable in an engine well past retirement age, were not good for one's blood pressure: cutting out in front of the Dartmouth ferry; refusing to start, even when warm, as a failing wind and a strengthening tide were setting us perilously close to some evil-looking reefs off L'Abervrac'h; and stalling without due notice, just as I'd slipped into reverse in a crowded lock where a brisk tail wind was keeping us going at a good 3 knots.

Our old Ford WaterMota was a four cylinder petrol engine, a robust and well-marinised machine based on the Anglia 105E block. I was never really sure of either its rated or actual power. One of the engineers at WaterMota once quoted me 12 old horsepower, which was always slightly puzzling. The Anglia car manual, passed on by the previous owner, listed the auto version of the 105E at 29 bhp, but we could never run at anything like the revs at which this output would have applied.

My feeling had always been that we could squeeze about 15 hp from the installation. *Stormalong* has a heavy displacement hull and normally motored at 4–4½ knots at economical cruising revs, just about reaching 6 knots for short bursts if necessary with everything wide open. We seemed to have plenty of thrust for manoeuvring. There was always a powerful no-nonsense propeller wash as I nudged ahead, and a reassuring 'bite' and swirling alongside as soon as we went astern. I wanted to retain this sense of having power ready, which is important when you are trying to turn a long-keeled boat in a marina and your neighbours are watching the 6 feet of bowsprit with undisguised apprehension.

The new engine would be diesel, for increased safety, economy, convenience and a longer cruising range, although I had defended our petrol WaterMota staunchly in many a saloon debate. It had run quietly with hardly any vibration, and I'm sure this is much appreciated by any wooden hull of a certain age, however strongly built.

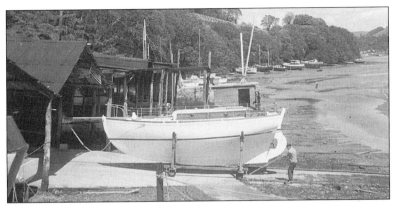

Stormalong hauled out at Creekside Boatyard, Dartmouth. *Photo by Jack Cumberlidge.*

Until the last couple of years, starting had invariably been reliable and instantaneous. Maintenance had been familiar and straightforward, and I'd always felt at ease tinkering around with spark-plugs, points and carburettor jets. Diesels, despite being much simpler than petrol engines, somehow seem more mysterious and not quite so homely.

So what sort of diesel were we looking for? Ideally, I suppose, one that would fit neatly into the same engine space, connect up to the same sterngear, run as smoothly and quietly as the old engine, deliver a few more horsepower so that we could cruise comfortably at just under hull speed, and not cost an arm and a leg. Bit of a tall order, but you've got to start somewhere.

This broad specification probably suggested a fairly fast-revving compact unit rather than a slow turning thumper – even though I'd always been impressed by traditional marine diesels such as Bukh, which had decompression levers and proper heavy flywheels, sounded like boat engines ought to sound, and yet were remarkably vibration-free. I'd used the 20 hp twin-cylinder Bukh aboard various other boats and had found it a thorough-going workhorse.

My initial thoughts tended towards a four-cylinder engine that might fit reasonably closely onto the old engine beds and line up with the existing shaft coupling without too much juggling about. However, given that the old engine was definitely coming out, it seemed a good idea to cast the net wide and weigh up all possible contenders, some of which would incorporate the most recent advances in small diesel design.

◆ WORKING OUT OPTIMUM HORSEPOWER

This is a logical and instructive starting point when choosing a new engine from scratch, even if you think you already know what size unit your boat needs. It doesn't take long for discussions about power to become quite involved, since there's rather more to the subject than first meets the eye. In general terms, though, power is the rate at which an engine is able to do the work required of it. For those who like to define their terms, 1 hp is equal to 550 foot-pounds of work per second, a foot-pound being the work extended to lift a weight of one pound through a distance of one foot. Power can also be expressed metrically in kilowatts, with 1 hp equivalent to 0.746 kw.

The important point to appreciate about power measurements as they appear in engine manufacturers' specifications is that power is always quoted with respect to a given engine speed – normally measured in revolutions per minute (rpm). Therefore when a brochure talks about a 20 hp engine, it usually means that the engine can deliver 20 hp at its maximum rated speed, which for small marine diesels may be somewhere between 3000 and 3600 rpm. This maximum output can be quoted as gross (or brake) horsepower from the engine *without* its transmission, or as net power (slightly less than the gross horsepower) – which is the usable power at the output side of the reduction/reversing gearbox.

Brochures often contain simple graphs showing power output plotted against rpm. These curves are important when you are choosing an engine, because you'll need to assess the horsepower available at your likely cruising revs – which will be rather less than the maximum quoted power. Firstly, you have to estimate how much horsepower will be needed, wherever it finally comes from, to drive your boat at the required cruising speed.

Estimating power required for a given speed

Displacement boats have a natural maximum hull speed, which is a function of their waterline length. If Sh is the maximum hull speed in knots and WL your waterline length in feet, then:

$Sh = 1.4 \times \sqrt{WL}$ approximately   Formula 1

Since *Stormalong's* waterline length is 26.6 ft, her maximum hull speed is given by:

$Sh = 1.4 \times \sqrt{26.6} = 7.2$ knots

If excess horsepower tries to push a displacement hull beyond its theoretical maximum speed, the boat will try, in effect, to climb over her own bow wave, tucking her stern right down and creating a large and inefficient wash. A wooden hull, in particular, will be subject to considerable extra strain under such conditions.

Therefore, for practical purposes you'll probably want to decide upon an occasional maximum speed a little below the hull speed – say 6½ knots for *Stormalong* – and then a comfortable cruising speed a little below that, which I reckoned at 5½–6 knots. The problem then is to work out the horsepower required to achieve these speeds and allow a reasonable reserve of power in hand.

Ideally, the most accurate way to assess required horsepower would be somehow to measure the water and air resistance offered by your particular boat at a given working maximum speed and then select an engine and propeller combination that would generate that amount of thrust. However, measuring or calculating resistance is a difficult business. For yachts and small commercial vessels, in practice it's simpler and sufficiently accurate to use one of the graphs, tables or formulae that have been refined over the years to relate *displacement* to boat speed and required horsepower. One such formula for displacement hulls is:

$$\frac{S}{\sqrt{WL}} = 10.665 \div \sqrt[3]{(D/shp)} \qquad \text{Formula 2}$$

where WL is the waterline length as before, D the displacement in pounds, and shp is the shaft horsepower (ie the power actually transmitted to the propeller) needed to achieve a given speed S.

The left-hand side of this formula, the ratio $S/\sqrt{WL}$, is often referred to in graphs and tables as the speed–length ratio. For older boats, of course, displacement is still the trickiest part of the equation to complete. It is relatively easy to work out Thames tonnage or registered tonnage, for example (both of which are quite crude measures of capacity and can be computed after some careful work with a tape measure), but displacement (ie how much your boat actually weighs) is a different matter altogether.

Owners of more recently built boats, especially class boats, can usually contact the builder or designer to obtain a reasonably accurate figure for basic hull displacement. For boats like *Stormalong*, there are methods for measuring the lines of the hull when she is chocked up in order to arrive at a good approximation for displacement. Such procedures are quite laborious though, and most boatowners will probably find themselves resorting to an informed guesstimate.

To your basic hull displacement, however you obtain it, must be added the weight of the engine, an estimate of the weight of crew, gear and stores that would normally be carried aboard, and the weight of, say, two-thirds the total tankage of fuel and water. After I had sat down and made some calculations I eventually arrived at a plausible figure of 6 tons for *Stormalong's* total displacement.

Taking my working maximum speed of 6½ knots, converting the displacement into pounds and inserting these values into the above formula, gives the required shaft horsepower, shp, expressed by:

$$\frac{6.5}{\sqrt{26.6}} = 10.665 \div \sqrt[3]{(13440/\text{shp})}$$

$$0.1182 = \frac{1}{\sqrt[3]{(13440/\text{shp})}}$$

$$0.001651 = \frac{\text{shp}}{13440}$$

Therefore shp=0.001651 x 13440=22.2 hp

This formula thus indicates that *Stormalong's* new engine would have to deliver 22.2 hp at the propeller in order to drive her 6 ton displacement hull at 6.5 knots in calm conditions. It is usually reasonable to assume a 3 per cent power loss through the gearbox and another 3 per cent loss through the sterngear bearings, in which case the brake horsepower, bhp, for this working maximum speed would be given by:

bhp x 94% = 22.2
So that bhp = 23.6 hp

The question now is: how much power should you have in reserve for adverse weather, missing a tide, tricky manoeuvres, taking avoiding action in a hurry or other contingencies? This can be a difficult compromise because while most cruising yachtsmen these days would avoid under-powering their boats, it is also important not to overpower. Apart from the obvious wasteful consequences such as unnecessarily high purchase and running costs, excess weight, the loss of usable space on board, and so on, you must also bear in mind that it is not good for diesel engines to be underworked. On the contrary, they thrive on being run near the upper end of their designed speed range.

For most of the time, ie when driving your boat at her normal cruising speed, a marine diesel should be running at not less than about 75 per cent of its maximum rated revs. Therefore, if you install an engine that is too powerful for your hull, it will be underworking at less-than-ideal revs for much of its life. This will eventually result in glazed cylinders, loss of compression, excessive smoking, and heavy oil consumption. As a rule of thumb, it is usually reckoned that for a displacement sailing boat at least, your maximum engine power should not be more than 10 per cent greater than that needed to drive the hull at her occasional maximum speed. Applying this rule to *Stormalong*, it looked as though we should be considering engines rated at around 26 bhp.

When you come to compare different engine specifications, it is also important to work out the shaft horsepower required to achieve your intended *normal cruising speed*. You can then enter this figure into each engine's output curve of horsepower against rpm, to check that the revs required to deliver your 'cruising horsepower' would not be less than 75 per cent of the maximum rated revs. For *Stormalong*, for example, the theoretical power needed to give a 6 knot cruising speed *in calm conditions* worked out at 18.6 hp, using formula 2 and allowing for transmission loss as before. We used this cruising horsepower to compare the output curves of various engines identified as possible contenders.

◆ CHOOSING AN ENGINE

Nowadays, the market is well served with an impressive choice of small marine diesels, and most manufacturers offer a wide range of sizes in which the horsepowers are usefully spaced. They all seem rather expensive by the time you have totted everything up and included VAT, but if you buy wisely, make a good job of the installation, and are conscientious about maintenance, you can expect a long working life in return. The table shown in Fig 1.1 gives the basic details of those engines between 24 hp and 33 hp that I seriously considered for *Stormalong*. This list is not exhaustive, but it nevertheless covers a fair spread from the market leaders to the smaller manufacturers.

Eventually, having studied many brochures and investigated most of the engine stands at the Southampton and London boat shows, I was able to refine my criteria for making a considered choice.

Fig 1.1 Engine comparison table (engines listed in alphabetical order).

	Max engine dimensions excluding mounts L W H	Space (m²) taken up in engine box	Net weight with standard gearbox (kg)	BHP	Max rpm	No of cyls	ccs	Type of cooling F = fresh D = direct O = option
Beta Marine BD1005	774 475 637	0.234	150	28	3600	3	1001	F
Bukh DV24ME (direct cooled)	786 470 640	0.236	210	24	3600	2	964	D
Lister LPW3 or LPWS3	867 515 600	0.268	180	30	3000	3	1395	F
Lombardini LDW 1003M	636 488 522	0.162	115	30	3600	3	1028	F
Nanni 3.100 HE	742 482 594	0.212	130	29	3600	3	1001	F
Solé Mini 26	723 480 503	0.175	112	25	3600	3	952	F
Vetus M 3.09	715 450 500	0.161	123	25	3600	3	952	F
Volvo Penta D1-30	728 482 553	0.194	145	28.4	3200	3	1130	F
Westerbeke 30B	750 508 516	0.197	124	27	3600	3	1000	F
Yanmar 3YM30	716 462 545	0.180	133	30	3600	3	1115	F

Our saloon hatch is quite narrow so there were tight limits on the physical size of engine which could be eased down below.

Physical size and weight

I was keen to use more or less the same engine space under the bridgedeck and avoid making too many structural alterations. If the new engine was physically smaller than the old WaterMota, we would have room to improve the all-round access and also make an efficient job of sound-proofing the engine compartment. There was also quite a tight limit on the physical size of machine we could manoeuvre down through the saloon hatch, which was only 630 mm (just over 2 ft) wide.

I wanted to minimise the weight of the new installation as far as possible. Although *Stormalong* has a displacement hull that seems to absorb extra weight without drastic effect, every year we seem to be adding things on board rather than taking them away. Even though we were moving from petrol to diesel, I was hoping not to increase the weight of the engine and equipment – and perhaps even decrease it.

Slow or high revving? How many cylinders?

Much as I like the idea, and the sound, of a slow-turning heavy-duty diesel, there are now very few on the market in *Stormalong's* horsepower range. In any case, I'm sure that a comparatively fast-revving engine, on good flexible mounts, is much kinder to an elderly wooden hull than a more traditional 'thumper'.

I was also beginning to favour a three-cylinder engine as likely to give the best balance between compactness and smooth running. Twins, on the whole, are still more subject to vibration at lower revs, however well counterbalanced they may be, while most four-cylinder engines I looked at were a little too powerful for our needs.

Compatibility with existing sterngear

If the new engine was to line up with the existing propeller shaft, it had to have a low-profile oil sump. This was because the old WaterMota was fitted with a dropped reduction gearbox which allowed the engine itself to be mounted fairly high in its compartment while the output half-coupling stepped down to meet the propeller shaft. The reduction gear for the new engine would almost certainly be integral with its gearbox, so the whole unit would have to sit much lower in the compartment than before. Retaining the same basic sterngear also meant using the same diameter propeller shaft. The old shaft was 28 mm (1⅛ in) diameter bronze, so we had to be sure that the output torque from the new engine could be safely transmitted by a new stainless steel shaft of 28 mm (1⅛ in) diameter.

All the engineers I talked to about this seemed to think that a 28 mm (1⅛ in) diameter stainless steel shaft was more than adequate for the maximum of 30 hp that we had in mind. One or two said that we might get away with using the old bronze shaft, but this seemed a bit dubious and, in any case, would only be feasible if the new shaft length was the same or shorter than the old one.

Fig 1.2 shows a commonly used graph for calculating the size of propeller shaft for a given shaft horsepower at a specified propeller speed. The degree of reduction provided by the gearbox is obviously important, because the greater the reduction, the greater the maximum torque that can be applied to the shaft, and the stronger it needs to be.

The graph is entered on the left-hand scale with maximum shaft horsepower per 100 revs of propeller speed. Since we were probably going to fit an engine of between 26 bhp and 29 bhp, the maximum shaft horsepower – allowing for a 6 per cent power loss through the gearbox and sterngear – would be 28 shp in round figures. With a likely reduction ratio of 2:1 and maximum engine revs of 3600 rpm (from Fig 1.1) our maximum propeller speed would be 1800 rpm. The shaft horsepower per 100 revs of propeller speed would therefore be: $28 \div 18 = 1.56$.

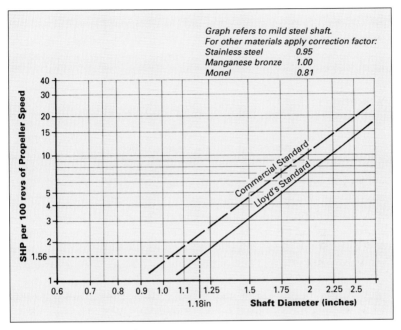

Graph refers to mild steel shaft.
For other materials apply correction factor:
Stainless steel   0.95
Manganese bronze   1.00
Monel   0.81

Fig 1.2 Calculating safe shaft diameter.

Entering 1.56 on the left-hand scale of Fig 1.2 and then following across to the Lloyd's Standard graph for a tail shaft gives a nominal shaft diameter, read off from the bottom scale, of 1.18 in. A factor of 0.95 is then applied if the shaft is of stainless steel. Multiplying 1.18 by 0.95 gives 1.12, so a shaft of 1⅛ in diameter (1.125 in) would do nicely. Our old bronze shaft would be just about satisfactory if we slipped a shade below Lloyd's Standard.

We would almost certainly need a new propeller, though. Quite apart from the importance of carefully matching a propeller to a particular engine and hull, our old propeller was left-handed, while most modern engines require one that is right-handed.

Cost of spares

The cost of marine engine spares is a well-aired subject in the yachting magazines, but bear in mind that the marine market is small compared with the automotive market – and the much lower turnover of marine spare parts must mean higher prices than car manufacturers can charge. For basic marine engine spares, though, there's not that much difference between manufacturers. When you are comparing engine prices, it's also worth asking about each manufacturer's price for a basic set of the three most common on-board spares – an alternator drive-belt, a water pump impeller, and an oil filter.

Ease of servicing

Slowly but surely, manufacturers are taking account of the fact that marine engines are usually installed in tiny compartments with limited room for daily checks and regular maintenance. The trend is to keep at least the engine oil dipstick, the oil filler and the fresh-water filler accessible towards the forward end of the engine, but there are still eccentric variations to be found.

With *Stormalong*'s own engine compartment in mind, I examined the various engines on the list to see where these components were mounted. I also located the oil filter, any engine-mounted fuel filters, the adjustment for the alternator belt, and the cold start button if fitted. The latter are normally used on direct injected diesels, and there needs to be a convenient system for remote control by cable. Indirectly injected diesels are fitted with glow plugs for cold starting, which are easily operated by turning the starter key to an intermediate position.

To clarify these terms, with direct injection the diesel is injected straight into the top of the cylinder just above the piston. With indirect injection the engine has a precombustion chamber (sometimes called a 'swirl chamber') alongside each cylinder, but connected to it. The precombustion chamber comes under compression with the rest of the cylinder as the piston reaches top dead centre. The injector then squirts a fine spray of diesel into the chamber and the gases expand back into the cylinder to cause the down stroke. Because this expansion is more controlled with indirect injection, these engines tend to be quieter and smoother running than direct injected engines. However, direct injection is more economical on fuel and usually makes for easier starting at low temperatures.

To simplify oil changes, I was looking for an accessible sump pump connection, although some engines had a pump permanently mounted. And how easy would it be to top up and change the gearbox oil? Most gearboxes can only be emptied through a drain plug right at the bottom of the casing, so you need to allow room to get some kind of container or plastic bag underneath.

◆ REVIEW OF ENGINES

Our original choice

When we bought and installed our Perkins Perama M30 back in 1990, it was the most competitively priced and one of the most compact small diesels available. The Perama had a very low-profile sump, good access to dipstick, oil and water fillers, and (for our particular engine compartment) to the oil filter and sump pump connection. We were impressed by the quiet, smooth running throughout the rev range, and I was also influenced by the fact that Perkins have a solid reputation, a worldwide distributor network and realistically priced spares.

Perkins was one of the first engine manufacturers to offer a three-cylinder, smooth-running, relatively fast-revving marina diesel based on a Japanese block. This trend continued steadily, so that now most of the smaller marine diesels, certainly up to 30–35 hp, are based on engines produced by Mitsubishi or Kubota. Notable exceptions are the Danish manufacturer Bukh, who make their own engines, and Volvo Penta, whose smaller blocks are supplied by Perkins.

Since our Perkins Perama was installed, the quality, performance and specification of all marine diesels has continued to improve steadily, while at the same time competition has kept prices keen in real terms. Deciding on a new 25–30 hp engine for *Stormalong* now would be even more difficult than it was in 1990, because all the engines in my comparison list below are excellent in technical terms. To some extent your decision will turn significantly on physical size, the price you can negotiate and the kind of personal brand preference that's always impossible to quantify but is nonetheless important in this kind of purchase. However, as an aid to decision-making, I have set out below my own reactions to each of the engines that would be in my comparison list if I were renewing our engine now.

BETA MARINE BD1005

The range of marine diesels offered by Beta Marine has increased steadily in the past ten years and Beta have grown to become a highly respected manufacturer with an extensive network of agents. Value for money has always been their watchword, but they are well up with all the longer established manufacturers in terms of quality of build and specification. Beta are also good at highly practical design features and innovations. For example, I like the neat way in which the electrical connections are made to their engines through heavy-duty terminals. Their easily accessible alternator mountings also allow for simple belt adjustment, which certainly turned out not to be the case with our Perkins Perama. I would say that, of all the manufacturers, Beta Marine probably have the most practical understanding of how their engines are actually fitted and used in the tight confines of a boat's engine compartment.

BUKH DV24ME (DIRECT COOLED)

We could probably have managed with 24 bhp for *Stormalong*, although I was keen to have enough power in reserve for those occasions when it really counts. Bukh were one of the first manufacturers to use sophisticated counterbalancing to minimise vibration, so the direct injected DV24 is extremely smooth-running despite being a twin. Bukh engines are also very ruggedly built and the raised hand starting facility is a practical feature. I wouldn't have begrudged the price of this workmanlike engine, but on balance the DV24 was physically a bit large, its sump not as low-profile as some, and the power a little on the light side.

LISTER LPW3 OR LPWS3

This three-cylinder workhorse is a fairly hefty unit for its 30 bhp and is both physically larger and heavier than I would probably consider for *Stormalong*. On the plus side, this strongly built, low-maintenance engine is well suited to those long periods of neglect or 'unattention' most yacht auxiliaries receive in practice.

The LPW3 is a direct injected engine with excellent fuel consumption, while the LPWS3 is indirect injected and has glow-plug heaters for cold starting. It's worth considering that Listers are not converted automotive engines but are conceived and designed as marine engines so that, for example, both the LPW3 and LPWS3 have solid crankcase door access rather than flimsy sumps. This makes the bottom of the engines very solid and durable in the often damp and potentially corrosive environment of a yacht bilge. These engines also have hydraulic, self-adjusting tappets that need no maintenance and result in very quiet valve gear.

LOMBARDINI LDW 1003M

Lombardini engines are built in Italy and distributed in the UK by Golden Arrow Marine of Poole. Fairways Marine Engineers of Colchester are useful local agents. On first sight, Lombardini engines look slightly unusual and the three-cylinder 30 hp 1003M seems unexpectedly short, squat and almost cubic in shape. This is partly because Lombardini have developed their own, patented fuel injection system, in which the injection pump is an integral part of the cylinder head. The whole design of the engine is more compact, so you won't see any of those familiar fuel pipes between high-pressure pump and injectors. Lombardini claim that this system provides more precise and consistent injection timing, leading to improved performance, leaner fuel consumption and cleaner exhaust emissions. I have no experience of using Lombardini engines and can't really evaluate these claimed benefits, but although you don't see that many Lombardinis aboard boats in the UK, they are widely used in the Mediterranean by fishing boats as well as yachts. Certainly if you are looking for a particularly short engine around 30 hp, then the 1003M is an interesting contender.

NANNI 3.100 HE

These engines are assembled in France on a Japanese (Kubota) block and distributed in the UK by A R Peachment of Brundall, near Norwich, who are excellent engineers. The 3.110 HE is a three-cylinder indirect injected engine giving 27 bhp at 3000 rpm. At 130 kg the Nanni is one of the lightest engines in the current comparison list, but doesn't have quite such a low-profile sump as some of the others. Good alternator access for belt adjustment.

SOLÉ MINI 26

This very neat looking three-cylinder diesel has a maximum output of 25 hp at 3600 rpm. Marinised in Spain and based on a well-proven Mitsubishi engine, the Solé Mini 26 is a couple of inches longer than our original Perkins Perama but a shade lower. At 112 kg it was also, and still is, the lightest engine in the comparison list. Its low profile sump is similar to the Perama's and at the time we were trying to decide on a new engine the Solé was a serious contender, although slightly light on power for *Stormalong's* heavy hull. Solé engines are distributed in the UK by Fairways Marine Engineers of Colchester.

VETUS M 3.09

I like much of the Vetus equipment and their Mitsubishi based engines are robust, well designed and nicely uncluttered. Vetus also offer an excellent waterproof instrument panel that has a useful battery voltmeter and includes an engine hour-meter on the tachometer. The Vetus M 3.09 is the lowest and one of the most compact engines in the comparison list. It would be a serious contender if we were changing our engine now, although with a maximum output of 24 hp at the shaft not quite as powerful as I'd prefer for *Stormalong*'s heavy hull. The next Vetus size up, the four-cylinder M 4.14, would be a bit too powerful for us at 33 bhp.

VOLVO PENTA D1-30

We are now up at the expensive end of the list, but it can't be denied that Volvo-Penta are among the most well developed of marine engines. Volvo sometimes come under fire for their alleged high price of spares, but they maintain an excellent worldwide service network, good stocks of parts and can supply a wide range of accessories. The 28 bhp of the direct injected D1-30 would be just right for *Stormalong* and I like the fact that this power is produced at relatively low cruising rpm. Although I haven't given decibel ratings for any of the engines, I suspect the Volvo D1-30 is one of the quietest engines in the list at normal cruising speed. The standard 115 amp alternator gives a generous charging rate.

WESTERBEKE 30B

I liked the look of this indirect-injected three-cylinder American engine, distributed in the UK by WaterMota Ltd. It has a fairly low profile sump and takes up less overall space than any contender on the list. The Westerbeke 30B weighs in at only 125 kg, is 2½ inches longer than our Perkins Perama, a shade narrower and a couple of inches lower. I like the optional 'Admiral' control panel, which has oil pressure and water temperature gauges, a battery charge rate voltmeter and a tachometer with an engine-hour meter.

YANMAR 3YM30

A three-cylinder indirect injected engine with the right output – 27 bhp at 3600. Although it has a low-profile sump, the Yanmar 3YM30 is not notably compact overall. The main dipstick is well back and quite low down. Yanmar engines are undoubtedly popular and have a good reputation for reliability and value for money, but I have to confess to being slightly prejudiced against them, especially the Yanmars towards the smaller end of the range. Some of those I've used in the past sounded like a bag of marbles at low revs, especially when cold. I also find the design and layout rather cluttered, especially when you compare the Yanmar 3YM30 with, say, the Vetus M 3.09.

Installing a new engine | 2

When you lift an old engine out of a boat and contemplate the grimy space left behind, with its motley array of bent copper pipes and tangled electrics, it can be difficult to imagine the same compartment clean and tidy, occupied by gleaming new machinery, its fuel lines and wires neatly clipped to bulkheads. As we hoisted our elderly Ford WaterMota up through the hatch for the last time, the general clutter of the old installation looked a daunting prospect. It would be a while before our new diesel engine was standing there, all connected up and ready to go.

We would need a new fuel tank, because the old brass tank would not be suitable for diesel. The Vetus exhaust system, fitted eight years ago, would probably have to be renewed with the next size up, from 40 mm (just over 1½ in) in 50 mm (just under 2 in) diameter. The existing inlet seacock for the raw cooling water was also on the small side and would have to be changed for a larger fitting that allowed a faster rate of flow.

The WaterMota had been solidly mounted on wooden bearers, which had been coach-screwed, somewhat crudely, to a pair of main frames on each side of the hull. The old reduction gearbox had stepped well down below the engine to meet the propeller shaft, whereas the output coupling from the Hurth gearbox on the new Perkins Perama finished up just above the level of the low-profile sump. We would have to start from scratch with the bearers, even if the originals had been better engineered in the first place.

◆ DESIGNING NEW ENGINE BEARERS

Engine bearers need to be just as immovable for a flexibly mounted engine as for a solidly mounted one. They need to be rigid enough to keep engine and shaft aligned and strong enough to withstand engine vibration, engine torque, propeller thrust and considerable acceleration forces in rough sea conditions. The rapid change of velocity as a boat pitches and rolls can reach the equivalent of about '8 g', which means that an engine could impose working loads on its mountings of eight times its own weight. The Perama weighs 133 kg (293 lb), which meant that our new bearers might have to cope with 1064 kg (2344 lb) (ie something over a ton) as a matter of course.

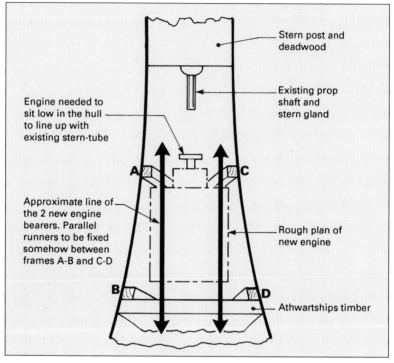

Fig 2.1 Rough plan of engine compartment with useful strong-points A, B, C, D.

Stormalong is well endowed with substantial oak frames, so we had a good sturdy base to work from. As with most modern engines, the Perama's mounting points form a perfect rectangle on the same plane, so the obvious arrangement for new bearers is usually two parallel fore-and-aft runners of some kind, strongly fixed to the hull. Space was tight athwartships for the aft mounts, because the engine had to sit well down near the turn of the bilge to line up with the existing shaft (see Fig 2.1). Rather than trying to squeeze in bulky timber runners, we decided to use two lengths of 8 mm (just over ¼ in) angle-iron, bolted in some way between two adjacent pairs of frames. Angle-iron is immensely strong and easy to work, and can be galvanised to give excellent protection against rust.

It seems as if all bolts turn out to be oddly shaped when you are planning modifications, but timber boats of a certain age are less symmetric than most. The two pairs of frames on either side of the engine compartment were not quite the same distance apart, and neither did the port and starboard side frames seem equidistant from the engine driveline – an imaginary axis projected forwards along the direction of the propeller shaft.

This driveline is one of the first measurements to establish when you are installing a new engine and hoping to use the existing sterngear as far as possible. The propeller tube, with its shaft bearing at the outboard end and sterngland at the inner, can be quite a job to change on a wooden boat, so most owners try to leave this alone if everything is working properly. In this case, the projected line of the existing propeller shaft will determine where the engine has to be mounted within its compartment.

The driveline needs to be carefully measured to within about 5 mm (just under ¼in) vertically and horizontally. Although there will be some scope for adjustment using the flexible mounts, life is easier if the engine bearers end up as close as you can get them to their correct position. It is obviously better to err on the side of having the bearers too low rather than too high, because you can always add a bit of height by fitting hardwood spacers under the mounts.

However, despite the fact that the engine can be raised or lowered on each of its flexible mounts using an adjusting nut, it is bad practice to 'jack up' the engine in this way. The higher the engine is sitting on its mounts, the more it tends to wobble about like a clown on stilts and the more vibration you will get at low revs or when rolling in a heavy sea. Ideally, the engine should be sitting as low down as possible on each mount, with perhaps one or two of the adjusting nuts raised just a little for fine tuning the alignment.

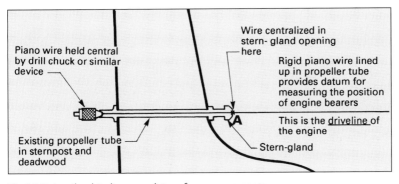

Fig 2.2 Using the driveline as a datum for measurements.

When you are working out how to construct new engine bearers, it is useful to set up the driveline using a straight length of wire (piano wire is ideal), as shown in Fig 2.2. If the boat is out of the water and the shaft drawn, the outboard end of the wire can be centred in the propeller tube using a drill chuck or similar clamping device. The wire is then led through to the engine space and held tight in position by any convenient means so that it emerges dead in the centre of the forward end of the propeller shaft – ie at point A in Fig 2.2. The wire thus represents the driveline and becomes the datum for all measurements affecting the bearers.

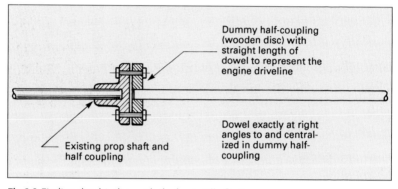

Fig 2.3 Finding the driveline with the boat still afloat.

Stormalong was moored in a tide berth when we were installing the engine, so the propeller shaft was in place most of the time. We therefore set up the driveline using a straight length of dowel, carefully jointed in the centre of, and at right angles to, a dummy half-coupling. This dummy was bolted to the propeller coupling and could easily be removed or replaced as required (see Fig 2.3).

When taking measurements, remember that flexible mounts compress with the weight of the engine, so their bearing surfaces end up in a lower position than when they are not supporting the engine. Our mounts could be compressed by between 0 and 10 mm with the boat pitching and rolling, but the static compression was about 5 mm (just under ¼ in) – halfway between the unloaded and fully squeezed positions.

The photograph above shows the final arrangement of the engine bearers. The aft ends of the two parallel angle-iron runners were bolted to short angle-iron stubs welded at just the right angle to two 8 mm (⁵⁄₁₆ in) steel plates specially shaped to the profile of the aft pair of frames. These

Final installation of the new bearers.

plates were fixed to the frames with 10 mm (just over ⅜ in) stainless steel bolts and lock nuts. The forward ends of the runners were bolted to similar angle-iron stubs welded to a much larger plate, which in turn was bolted across the hull between the forward pair of frames. The final rectangular steel frame was very strong and became, in effect, a structural part of the hull.

The plates and runners were made to our drawings by a local metal fabricator. This work was carried out in several stages, as the plates had to be cut out and clamped to the frames before we could work out the correct positions and angles for the runner stubs. We made a wooden dummy for each stub so that the welder would get the angles exactly right. When all welding was finished, the plates and runners were hot-dip galvanised. The most time-consuming job was the careful measuring to make sure that each runner ended up the same distance either side of the driveline and parallel to it, and that both runners were at just the right height so that the propeller shaft and gearbox couplings could be exactly lined up when the engine was sitting on its flexible mounts.

You can see from the photograph that we fitted an Aquadrive constant velocity coupling between the gearbox and the propeller shaft, in order to avoid the need for minutely precise lining up, reduce any engine vibration

The forward cross plate which is bolted athwartships between the two main frames B and D in Fig 2.1. The parallel angle-iron bearers are bolted to the two stubs which have been welded to the cross plate. All the iron components were hot-dip galvanised.

The two individually shaped after bearer plates which were bolted to the main frames A and C in Fig 2.1. The after ends of the engine bearers were then bolted to the angle-iron stubs welded to the plates.

The complete galvanised engine bearer frame before final assembly, showing the forward cross plate, and the angle-iron bearers which bolt between them.

transmitted to the hull, and minimise wear on the gearbox and propeller shaft bearings. Because the Aquadrive uses a thrust bearing fixed to the main structure of the hull between the gearbox and sterngland, the flexible mounts are relieved of horizontal thrust and allowed to work as they should – up and down. I will be looking at the installation of an Aquadrive in the next chapter; however, for designing the engine bearers, we had to take into account the exact length of the Aquadrive unit, which determined the final position of the gearbox output coupling.

The two bearers should not only be parallel and equidistant from the driveline, but should each follow the same level along their length (ie a spirit level should stay horizontal as you hold it at right angles across the bearers and slide along them). Ideally, all four flexible mounts should be compressed to the same extent when the engine is bolted down (see Fig 2.4). This means that the engine has to finish up vertical in the

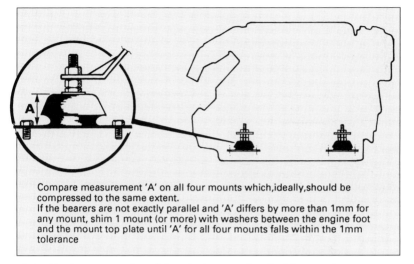

Compare measurement 'A' on all four mounts which,ideally,should be compressed to the same extent.
If the bearers are not exactly parallel and 'A' differs by more than 1mm for any mount, shim 1 mount (or more) with washers between the engine foot and the mount top plate until 'A' for all four mounts falls within the 1mm tolerance

Fig 2.4 The importance of parallel engine bearers when flexible mounting.

athwartships direction with the flexible mounts sharing the load evenly, as with the legs of a table. If the bearers are not quite parallel in both planes, so that one of the mounts is taking significantly more or less than its fair weight, you can suffer greatly increased vibration at low revs because of a 'three-legging' effect.

◆ NEW BEARERS IN GRP HULLS

Although the engine compartments in elderly wooden boats are often inconveniently shaped, installing new bearers is usually comparatively straightforward because you should have strong frames nearby to work to. A steel hull is also fairly easy to work with, since new brackets or bolting points can be welded wherever you need them. Fitting a new engine bed in a GRP hull, however, can be a major operation unless you can pick up on existing structures.

The main difficulties arise if you have to bond new strong points to the hull itself. The trick here is to ensure that the areas of GRP you are working to are absolutely clean and well prepared, so that new layers of glass and resin stand a good chance of bonding. Steam cleaning is useful to start with, in order to cut through the surface oil and ingrained grime. You then have a choice of tactics, depending on the size and shape of your engine compartment and *which* sort of discomfort you prefer!

A reliable way of preparing the surface is to disc sand until you get down to clean white laminate, using a fairly coarse disc of 80–120 grit. You must wear a mask for this job, because the polyester dust and fine particles of glass make an unpleasant combination.

An alternative is to use a heat gun and triangular scraper, heating the GRP carefully until the top layer goes soft and then scraping back evenly until you get down to a clean working surface that is uncontaminated by oil or grease. A third possibility, but one that I wouldn't recommend, is one of the methylene chloride-based chemical strippers. These solvents can be very savage unless used with extreme care, and they tend to spread dirt about rather than remove it.

Once you have a clean working surface, it can be worth applying a moisture-curing polyurethane primer – such as Bonda Marine G4 produced by Bondaglass-Voss – before starting the new laying up. This will effectively waterproof the area of GRP you have exposed and provide a good adhesive base for the fibreglass resin. You should start applying the resin and glass as soon as the G4 becomes finger tacky, normally within four hours of application in good drying conditions.

Production GRP engine bearers are often made up as two hollow 'tophat' sections filled with a suitable non-moisture-absorbing material. A mixture of sand and plastic is sometimes used to give the necessary weight and stability for damping vibration and hull-transmitted noise. However, this kind of filled structure is not so easy to achieve in a do-it-yourself installation, where it is more common for GRP bearers to be built up in layers over a core of hardwood (see Fig 2.5).

Reinforcement is provided by embedding two flat bar runners of

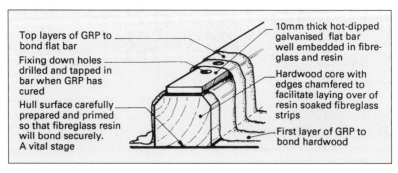

Top layers of GRP to bond flat bar

Fixing down holes drilled and tapped in bar when GRP has cured

Hull surface carefully prepared and primed so that fibreglass resin will bond securely. A vital stage

10mm thick hot-dipped galvanised flat bar well embedded in fibre-glass and resin

Hardwood core with edges chamfered to facilitate laying over of resin soaked fibreglass strips

First layer of GRP to bond hardwood

Fig 2.5 Making new GRP engine beds.

Our new Perkins Perama is finally lowered onto its bearings.

8–10 mm (⅜ in) stainless or galvanised steel along the top of the bearers. These distribute the engine load evenly and, once the GRP has fully cured, the bar can be drilled and tapped to take the fixing bolts for the flexible mounts.

◆ FUEL TANKS AND FILTERS

Stormalong's old cylindrical brass petrol tank was in reasonable condition, but we were advised to change it for either a mild steel or stainless steel tank. Diesel contains quite a high concentration of sulphur compounds, which over a lengthy period can react with zinc to corrode a brass tank. Galvanised tanks are not recommended for diesel, for the same reason.

We decided to have a new stainless steel tank made, similar in shape to the old one but a bit larger all round to give a few gallons' extra capacity, with a baffle plate to stop the diesel from surging about at sea and becoming aerated. For *Stormalong's* relatively small tank – 77 litres (17 gal) – the extra cost of stainless steel over mild steel was not all that great and well worth the advantage of not having to keep the tank painted.

Our tank is located on the port side of the cockpit above engine level, so diesel is effectively gravity fed to the low-pressure pump. The supply pipe has a brass tap at the tank and fuel is drawn from a couple of inches above a small water and sediment sump, which can be drained off with its own tap (see Fig 2.6). Next in line is a heavy-duty water separator mounted on a bulkhead in the engine compartment, and finally a cartridge-type fuel filter mounted on the engine itself.

A diesel engine needs a return pipe, which takes unused fuel from the high-pressure pump back to the tank. We used standard copper piping for the main supply and return, with armoured flexible pipe for the final connections to the engine. Our deck-filler is not connected directly to the tank, because I never really trust deck-filler caps to stay watertight. Instead,

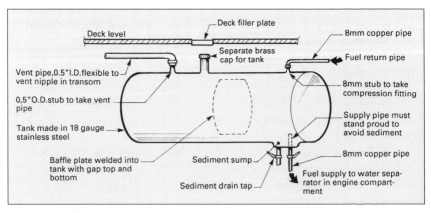

Fig 2.6 Fuel tank arrangement.

the tank has its own brass cap immediately under the deck-filler, which can easily be reached under the cockpit side. The tank is vented over the stern via a 12 mm (½ in) plastic pipe and a waterproof vent nipple fitted at the top of the transom.

The drain tap for the tank, the large-capacity water separator, and a good fuel filter are vital for a diesel installation. Accumulated water in the fuel – usually as a result of condensation – causes no end of problems in its own right, but can also encourage the growth of certain diesel bacteria known formally as *Cladosporium resinae*. These devilish microbes can flourish in any pocket of water that collects in the bottom of a tank. They feed off the diesel and multiply rapidly to form a sludge that will block your fuel pipes and filters, and play havoc with pressure pump and injectors if it gets that far.

Good housekeeping is important to keep the fuel system clean and efficient, so the installation should help to make life easy for drawing off moisture regularly from the bottom of the tank and from the water separator. Once bacteria start breeding anywhere in the system, they can be difficult to get rid of. Prevention is much easier than cure.

◆ EXHAUST SYSTEM

These days, fitting a new exhaust is fairly simple if you use the various fit-together components from well established suppliers. Vetus have probably been the most widely used, especially aboard smaller yachts, but Halyard (Marine & Industrial) Ltd now have a good range for all sizes of engine. Most marine exhausts are now water injected, so a typical set-up will look something like Fig 2.7, where the actual piping consists of steel reinforced rubber exhaust hose.

For a short exhaust run on a smallish engine you can sometimes dispense with the muffler, since the waterlock itself has quite good silencing properties, but the waterlock and gooseneck are key items in the chain. The waterlock collects all the water in the exhaust system when the engine is stopped, and the gooseneck prevents water entering the system through the outlet in a following sea.

The important point is that the diameter of the components and hose should be at least as wide as the diameter of the exhaust outlet from the engine, so that no significant back pressure can build up to detract from the performance of the engine. Our old engine had an exhaust outlet diameter of 40 mm (1½ in), whereas the exhaust diameter of the new Perama

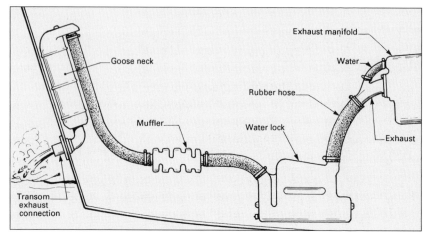

Fig 2.7 Water-injected exhaust system.

was 50 mm (2 in). We therefore renewed the complete system with 50 mm (2 in) hose, waterlock, muffler and gooseneck. It seemed extravagant at the time, but I was determined to avoid any shortcuts that might detract from the installation – and thus adversely affect the engine in the long run.

The exhaust was one of the last jobs in the installation, so that we could keep the space under the cockpit floor as clear as possible for running the electrics and engine control cables. Because of this, we didn't fully appreciate until quite late on that the exhaust outlet from the engine was too low in the compartment for the waterlock to be sited far enough below it – you need at least 30 cm (1 ft) to avoid the risk of cooling water swilling back into the manifold in a heavy sea.

This is a common installation problem with many modern engines, so most manufacturers – or their distributors – can supply a 'dry-riser', which is usually a short S-shaped length of steel pipe with two exhaust manifolds and the water injection bend (see Fig 2.8), effectively raising the exhaust outlet of the engine by about a foot so that the waterlock can be connected a safe distance below it.

With the Perama, we had to disconnect the injection bend from the manifold, connect in the dry-riser, and then devise a short pipe run to take the cooling water up to the bend in its new position. This meant reversing the original neoprene water outlet sleeve to point upwards, inserting a stub of copper pipe, and then fitting a short length of flexible radiator hose in an inverted U to the injection bend. Unfortunately, the cast stub that takes

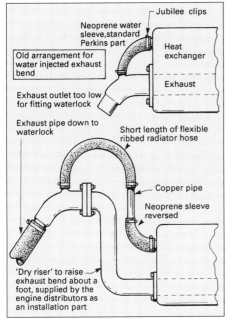

Fig 2.8 Fitting a 'dry-riser' to raise exhaust levels.

the water into the bend was slightly tapered and rather too short to take a hose clip safely. Therefore we had to do a further local modification and cut a thread on the outside to take a standard plumbing fitting.

If the injection point is near or below the waterline, there is the possibility, with the engine stopped, of raw cooling water siphoning through into the exhaust system, filling the waterlock and hose, and then trickling back through the manifold into the engine itself. In practice, the tight-fitting impeller in the raw-water pump can act as a temporary valve against the inflow of water when the engine is off, but it is still essential to take precautions against any risk of sea water in the engine.

The simplest remedy is to fit a siphon break valve a safe distance (a good 38 cm (15 in)) above the waterline between the pressure side of the raw-water pump and the inlet to the heat exchanger. The valve closes under pressure (ie when the engine is running), but falls open when the engine stops to break any potential siphon effect (see Fig 2.9).

Siphon break valves are available from various suppliers and some engine manufacturers produce their own. We used a Vetus 'air vent' valve installed 51 cm (20 in) above the waterline and as near the fore-and-aft line as possible. It was piped with two lengths of tough but flexible radiator

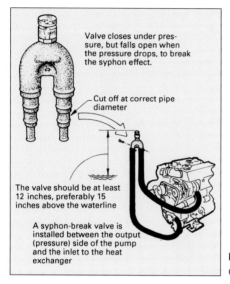

Valve closes under pressure, but falls open when the pressure drops, to break the syphon effect.

Cut off at correct pipe diameter

The valve should be at least 12 inches, preferably 15 inches above the waterline

A syphon-break valve is installed between the output (pressure) side of the pump and the inlet to the heat exchanger

Fig 2.9 Fitting a siphon break valve. *Courtesy of Vetus UK Ltd.*

hose and, although you can't actually see the valve operating, it contributes greatly to our peace of mind.

◆ WATER INLET SEACOCK AND STRAINER

The original water inlet seacock was a traditional bronze Stuart Turner type with an integral cylindrical filter. Unfortunately, this practical and workmanlike fitting only had a 12 mm (½ in) bore, whereas the Perama pump inlet has a 20 mm (approx. ¾ in) bore. It is asking for trouble to constrict the cooling water inlet, so we were obliged to exchange the seacock for one of larger diameter. Getting hold of a good solid inlet seacock with its own filter is not so easy these days, so we opted for a straightforward bronze skin-fitting from Vetus, with a scoopstrainer outside the hull and a thread-on seacock valve on the inside.

However, I like having a filter you can clean easily from inboard, so we fitted a Vetus waterstrainer between the seacock and the pump. This all-plastic component should be located at least 15 cm (6 in) above the waterline and has a wide transparent cover so that you can easily inspect the filter without taking the cap off. It is also reassuring to see the water bubbling through when the engine is running. I was somewhat prejudiced against this lightweight strainer after our 'proper' bronze seacock filter, but it has proved highly practical and trouble-free. The screw cap and actual strainer element are easy to remove for cleaning.

We installed the new skin-fitting in the same place as the old seacock, enlarging the hole in the hull slightly and bedding the fitting on Sikaflex. This is a first-class waterproof mastic, but rather expensive. However, if the inlet has to be relocated, give the matter some careful thought before you make a new hole in the hull. Work out how the hose has to lead to the water pump on the engine and try to site the new skin-fitting reasonably close to the water pump. It should not, though, be nearer than about a foot, so that the hose is long enough to flex with the movement of the engine. The seacock should obviously be easily accessible from inside, but as low down near the centreline as possible, so that water will draw with the boat well heeled on either tack.

◆ SOUND INSULATION

Effective sound installation is rather a specialist subject, and I soon discovered that there is a good deal more to obtaining a quiet installation than sticking a few pieces of foam around the engine compartment. Noise is a mysterious form of energy that can reverberate, amplify and bounce its way out through the smallest crevices. However, noise reduction is not just a matter of acoustics. To do a good job, you need to consider noise and vibration in the early stages of an installation and attack the problem on several fronts. Good solid engine beds, carefully set-up flexible mounts and sound engineering in the linkage between gearbox and propeller shaft all help to reduce the structure-borne vibration that can aggravate noise.

When using sound-insulation materials, the more you can arrange to enclose the engine with lined bulkheads and panels, the less noise will regenerate and ultimately escape into the saloon or up into the cockpit. This factor has an important bearing on where to mount fuel pipes and water separators, electrical function boxes, engine compartment lights, sterntube greasers, and any other auxiliary clutter that might prevent you from lining significant areas of bulkhead. Some careful thought is also required to run the fuel and water pipes, control cables and instrument wiring so that you don't end up with a network of 'noise escape routes' from the engine compartment.

Of course, the engine needs a clear supply of air for efficient combustion, but most small naturally aspirated diesels can easily draw enough breath through gaps to the equivalent of a 5 cm (2 in) diameter hole. If your compartment is enclosed meticulously, you may need to run a flexible air duct back to the cockpit – perhaps via a large vented locker. *Stormalong*'s engine compartment was never likely to be starved of air though, being open to the bilge and to the space immediately under the cockpit floor, which is not self-draining. To partly close off the installation from aft, we constructed an insulated 'baffle bulkhead' behind the engine; this does not by any means seal the compartment, but it significantly reduces the noise you hear from the cockpit.

When designing such additions, or planning the layout of the engine compartment generally, you need to take account of the physical thickness of the sound insulation material. We used the sophisticated multi-layer sound insulation supplied by Halyard Ltd, which is 32 mm (about 1¼ in) thick. This may not sound much, but it reduces the compartment volume quite considerably by the time you have this thickness each side and on top of the engine.

The insulation material has four distinct layers: a Marglass outer face, which is the tough grey material that you finally see around the engine compartment; a foam absorption layer, about 2½ cm (1 in) thick, which prevents noise from echoing round the compartment; a thin but dense layer of lead-loaded polymer, designed to stop noise dead; and finally, a 5 mm (just under ¼ in) layer of backed foam to isolate the leaded polymer from the bulkhead. The 86 cm x 61 cm (3 ft x 2 ft) sheets are fairly easy to cut to shape with a sharp Stanley knife, and most popular contact adhesives are suitable. Halyard recommend a thixotropic (jelly) adhesive such as Dunlop Thix-o-Fix.

I had opted for the rather more expensive 'fire zero-rated' insulation material, so that we finished up with an effective fire-resistant cordon round the engine that would considerably delay the spread of an engine compartment fire. Not all insulation material is fire zero-rated, but its extra cost seems fairly modest in the overall budget of a new installation.

We also used some of the Halyard self-adhesive hatch tape for making a tight seal round the removable parts of the engine box. You can tell that this makes a significant difference to the noise level in the saloon, because there is a marked increase in noise as soon as you lift the engine hatch just a little to separate the tape seal.

◆ GETTING IT ALL TOGETHER

There is a good deal of interdependence between the various operations involved in installing an engine, so you need to consider all stages from the outset and work out how they affect each other. In particular, watch out for the following hitches:

- Will the installation allow easy access to dipsticks, oil and fuel filters and oil drain plugs? In particular, make sure you can check and drain the gearbox oil without too much acrobatic contortion.
- Make sure there is enough sideways room to adjust the alternator belt tension as the belt stretches slightly.
- If you are changing from petrol to diesel, don't forget to provide for a fuel-return pipe back to the tank. Also, work out where best to site a tank vent nipple out in the open, but in a position not too exposed to water on deck.
- If the engine exhaust outlet is below or only just above the waterline, don't forget to fit a siphon break valve at least 38 cm (15 in) above the waterline on the pressure side of the water pump.
- Is there room to site the exhaust waterlock at least 30 cm (1 ft) below the engine exhaust outlet? If not, and you have to use a dry-riser, is there enough height in the engine compartment and how will you redirect the raw cooling water into the raised exhaust bend?

It is surprising just how long these auxiliary details take to work out, and how much they cost. Also, remember to order your equipment and materials in good time, because the weeks can easily drift by from the time you decide what size and type of item you need, find that it is out of stock, and eventually get it delivered. We all know the syndrome when chasing a vital component on a Saturday afternoon: 'If only you'd come in last week, sir. I can do you a 40 mm or a 60 mm left-handed. The 50 mm standards are on order – should be here in about a fortnight.'

3 | Transmission and sterngear

The business end of a marine engine – the final transmission and sterngear – can provide some of the most taxing installation problems for do-it-yourself engineers. When re-engining a boat with a unit of similar size and power, most owners will try to keep things simple by using as much of the existing sterngear as possible – even if this means redesigning the bearers to align the new engine. When fitting *Stormalong*'s new Perkins Perama, we needed a new propeller shaft and propeller, but it was feasible to keep the existing sterntube, sterngland and cutless bearing.

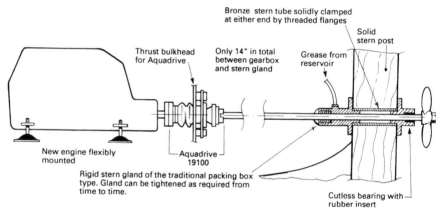

Bronze stern tube solidly clamped at either end by threaded flanges

Solid stern post

Thrust bulkhead for Aquadrive

Only 14″ in total between gearbox and stern gland

Grease from reservoir

New engine flexibly mounted

Aquadrive 19100

Rigid stern gland of the traditional packing box type. Gland can be tightened as required from time to time.

Cutless bearing with rubber insert

Fig 3.1 *Stormalong*'s sterngear.

Our basic sterngear, shown in Fig 3.1, is very traditional. The relatively short bronze sterntube passes through the deadwood and sternpost and is clamped solidly at either end by threaded flanges that are finally fixed to the hull by bronze screws at the inboard end and bronze catchbolts at the propeller end. The sterngland is of the old packing-box type, with an adjusting cup tightening on to three rings of graphited packing string. The manual sterntube greaser, which has a large reservoir, forces grease into the tube just behind the sterngland and then back down to the cutless bearing. The propeller shaft and cutless bearing are thus lubricated by a mixture of water and grease, which seems to keep things running smoothly. The propeller itself sits close to the sternpost in a moderate cavity cut from the rudder.

The shaft, which is only about 112 cm (44 in) long over all, is held rigid by the sterngland and cutless bearing. Because the old engine was solidly mounted, there was no requirement for a flexible coupling or a flexible gland. Since I was keen to leave our sterngear undisturbed, and simply replacing the old bronze shaft with the same diameter of stainless steel to cope with the extra torque of the Perama, we had to find some way of absorbing the play in the transmission introduced by flexibly mounting the new engine.

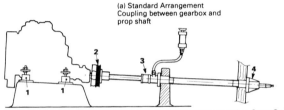

(a) Standard Arrangement
Coupling between gearbox and
prop shaft

1. Flexible Mounts. 2. Flexible Coupling. 3. Rigid Stern Gland. 4. Stern Cutless Bearing.

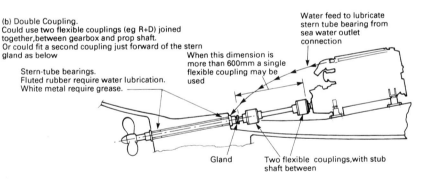

(b) Double Coupling.
Could use two flexible couplings (eg R+D) joined together,between gearbox and prop shaft.
Or could fit a second coupling just forward of the stern gland as below

Stern-tube bearings.
Fluted rubber require water lubrication.
White metal require grease.

Water feed to lubricate stern tube bearing from sea water outlet connection

When this dimension is more than 600mm a single flexible coupling may be used

Gland

Two flexible couplings,with stub shaft between

Fig 3.2 Flexible coupling.

◆ FLEXIBLE COUPLING

A flexible coupling is usually installed between the gearbox output flange and propeller shaft, as in Fig 3.2a, although where space allows you can sometimes fit a second coupling just forward of the sterngland (Fig 3.2b). There are various types of flexible coupling, although two of the most well-known suppliers are Vetus UK Ltd and R & D Marine Ltd. R & D Marine produce a polyurethane disc coupling which takes up very little fore-and-aft space, and two R & D couplings can be linked in series for the extra flex that may be needed when the length of shaft between gearbox and sterngland is relatively short. Vetus have a wide range of rubber-based flexible couplings, including Uniflex and Bullflex couplings that are said to cope with a permanent misalignment of up to 2 degrees between gearbox and propeller shaft.

As a general rule, though, a flexible coupling is not designed to absorb constant angular differences between gearbox and propeller shaft. The engine and shaft should be lined up just as accurately for flexible as for solid mounting, with the coupling only expected to cope with movement caused by natural flexing of the hull and the vibration of the engine on its flexible mounts. Even then, it can be easy to ask too much of flexible couplings in engineering terms. When you look at how some small single or twin-cylinder diesels jump about on their mounts at low revs, you can imagine the kind of stresses being applied to the gearbox and propeller shaft even when a good flexible coupling is fitted.

The dimensions of the propeller shaft provide certain constraints on the effectiveness of flexible coupling: the shaft diameter, its overall length, but particularly the distance between gearbox and sterngland. The latter measurement is only about 35 cm (14 in) for *Stormalong*, which allows little scope for any vibration. Our Perkins Perama is a very smooth running unit even at low revs, but it is easy to imagine how a standard flexible coupling, even doubled up, might not be pliable enough to cope with engine movement on such a tight leverage where the sterngland is rigidly fixed. With a diameter of about 27 mm (1⅛ in) in stainless steel, the propeller shaft itself would not be doing much flexing either.

◆ FLEXIBLE STERNGLAND AND 'FLOATING' SHAFT

Another way of providing some play in the system is to fit a flexible sterngland (Fig 3.3) that acts as a floating seal, so that the propeller shaft is only supported at each end (ie by the gearbox output flange and the outer cutless bearing). As the engine moves on its mounts or the hull flexes at sea, the shaft is then allowed a certain 'stirring' action which, with a reasonable length of shaft, the cutless bearing can safely accommodate. Some engine manufacturers supply their own flexible sternglands (often known as a stuffing-box) and self-aligning inner bearings, or you can buy workmanlike

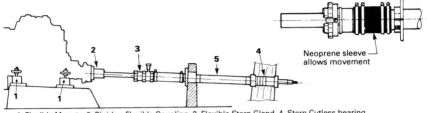

1. Flexible Mounts. 2. Rigid or Flexible Coupling. 3. Flexible Stern Gland. 4. Stern Cutless bearing.
5. Oversized Stern Tube

Fig 3.3 Using a flexible sterngland.

units off-the-shelf from various suppliers such as Lancing Marine, T Norris Ltd or Vetus UK Ltd.

◆ USING AN AQUADRIVE

Even if we were to fit a flexible sterngland, which I was not keen to do, *Stormalong's* short shaft would still limit quite considerably the amount the engine could be allowed to move. Because of this, I began to consider the pros and cons of fitting an Aquadrive, the heavy-duty coupling system supplied by Halyard Ltd. An Aquadrive comprises two sealed constant-velocity joints and an integral thrust bearing, providing fully engineered movement between gearbox and shaft. This solution would be more expensive than using a flexible coupling or flexible sterngland, but the advantages seemed highly attractive.

Considering that CV joints are used in car transmissions as a matter of course, I have often wondered why we seem prepared to put up with relatively crude drive systems aboard a boat, where engines and gearboxes are generally more expensive and difficult to repair, and the consequences of transmission failure can be rather more serious. By fitting a marine CV coupling such as an Aquadrive between the gearbox and propeller shaft, you remove the need for such minutely critical lining up between engine and transmission, and thus all the components of the system are able to do their job to best advantage.

The engine is free to vibrate on its flexible mounts, but hardly any of this vibration is transmitted via the shaft and sterntube to the hull. Because the propeller thrust is taken directly by the hull through the thrust bearing, the flexible mounts are able to work to full efficiency in a vertical plane, without being pushed forwards by the drive from the shaft.

The wear on the sterngear is greatly reduced, since there are no sideways forces on the propeller shaft and sterngland that even the best flexible couplings cannot help imparting. The engine and gearbox are well protected in the event of something nasty tangled round the propeller, because the thrust bearing should absorb most of the initial shock while the CV joints prevent any subsequent rough running from reaching the gearbox and engine.

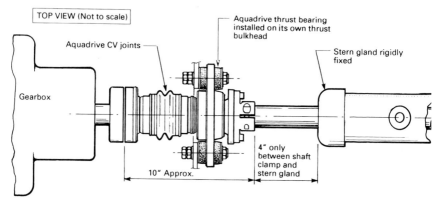

Fig 3.4a The original Aquadrive fitted in neatly between the gearbox and the sterngland.

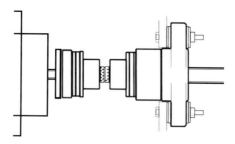

Fig 3.4b The smallest Aquadrive in the current range is the CVB 05.10, the unit we would have to fit now if replacing the original 19100. This drawing shows the slightly different configuration and increased length of the CVB 05.10.

The cost of these benefits would be some additional outlay and also the actual installation would be slightly more involved, because the Aquadrive needs its own support bulkhead that has to be man enough to take the thrust from the propeller. However, Fig 3.4 shows how the then 19100 Aquadrive which was the smallest in the range, fitted neatly between gearbox and sterngland, and the photograph on page 41 shows the unit mounted on its own mini-bulkhead of 10 mm (about ⅜ in) galvanised steel plate.

◆ INSTALLING THE AQUADRIVE

Two hardwood support blocks were carefully shaped to bolt just aft of the two main frames that support the aft engine bearer plates. The Aquadrive thrust bulkhead (see Fig 3.5) was bolted and coachscrewed to these blocks,

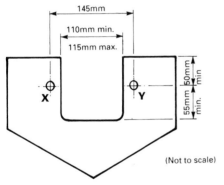

Thrust bearing support plate.
The unit is not supplied with a support plate. The material from which the plate is made can be varied - perhaps 10mm thick steel plate or 12mm plywood buried in at least 5 - 6 layers of GRP.
The important point is that the thrust bearing support plate must not flex under full thrust - i.e. it must be tough enough to push the boat along.

(Not to scale)

Fig 3.5a The Aquadrive thrust bulkhead.

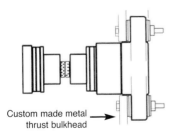

Custom made metal thrust bulkhead

Fig 3.5b Drawing of Aquadrive CVB 05.10 (the smallest in the current range) in relation to the thrust bulkhead.

whose careful shaping was necessary so that the bulkhead ended up just the right distance from the gearbox output flange and exactly parallel to it. Precise positioning of this bulkhead is important for best results. Obviously, the Aquadrive shaft clamp has to line up accurately with the propeller shaft, but also the Aquadrive itself should be coupled up so that the two CV joints are at, or very near, the midpoint of their horizontal float, ie neither too extended nor too compressed.

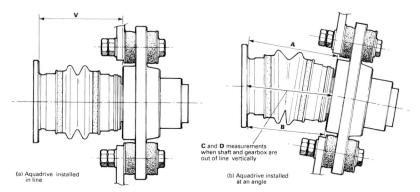

(a) Aquadrive installed in line

C and D measurements when shaft and gearbox are out of line vertically

(b) Aquadrive installed at an angle

Fig 3.6 The Aquadrive 'V' distance. It is important to get the Aquadrive 'V' distance right. For our original 19100, 'V' needed to be 112 mm plus or minus only 2 mm.

Fig 3.6a shows the important measurement for this requirement, distance 'V' in the installation instructions. Our 'V' distance had to be 112 mm ± 2 mm, a tolerance that required some care in designing and fitting the thrust bulkhead. Fig 3.6b shows how to calculate the 'V' distance as an average of measurements A and B, when the Aquadrive is installed at an angle, either intentionally or unintentionally. If the shaft and gearbox are at an angle horizontally as well as vertically, you have to measure A–D at each side as well as top and bottom of the Aquadrive, dividing by four to get the 'V' distance.

Connection to the gearbox flange was straightforward, using the standard adaptor kit for a Hurth HBW50 gearbox. At the aft end, the Aquadrive is connected to the propeller shaft using a shaft clamp. Having been brought up on woodruff keys and the like, I was initially a bit wary of the shaft clamp, but the system is accepted by Lloyd's and has proved to be completely sound. It is important, though, that shaft and clamp are accurately aligned and that the end of the shaft is machined to within 0.05

mm (0.002 in) of the nominal diameter of the clamp. The alignment needs to be just right when the Aquadrive is fitted to its thrust bulkhead, so you have to be very careful about marking and drilling the two holes X and Y in Fig 3.5. We drilled them when the bulkhead had been fitted to its final position, but not tightened in place.

With the clamp sliding smoothly on the shaft, the Aquadrive was moved forwards until the two thrust bearing bolts just touched the thrust bulkhead and then the two holes X and Y were accurately marked in this position. The holes were drilled and the plate sent for galvanising before the final installation.

The shaft clamp has a dimpling screw, as a precaution against slipping, for which you need to drill a shallow hole in the shaft using a 4 mm or 5 mm (5/32 in or 3/16 in) drill. This operation requires some care, both in measuring the position of the hole and in actually doing the drilling on a slippery machined shaft. The trick with the drilling is to make a small locating dinge with a fine centrepunch and drill this out a bit with a 1 mm (1/32 in) and then a 2 mm (1/16 in) drill before using the larger drill to make the main hole.

The original Aquadrive 19100 installed on a thrust bulkhead of 10 mm galvanised steel plate bolted to the main frames supporting the after bearer plates. Two hard-wood spacers adjust the distance between the Aquadrive and the gearbox. Note the shaft clamp with its dimpling screw, the sterngland greaser pipe and terminals for the zinc anode.

This installation picture of the current CVB 05.10 Aquadrive shows both the gearbox and thrust bulkhead connections.

Although the Aquadrive can cope quite happily with the engine and propeller shaft up to about 15 degrees out of line or up to 12 mm (½ in) displaced from each other, you obviously benefit from improved long-term wear if the whole lining up is as accurate as you can make it. As with any mechanical component, careful installation is the key to reliability and optimum performance.

The new transmission has worked well, with the Aquadrive isolating all engine movement from the propeller shaft and sterngear. You can put your hand on the sterngland with the engine driving ahead at cruising speed and feel not a flicker of vibration, which makes for a pleasantly quiet installation, minimal wear throughout the transmission, and a kindly effect on *Stormalong's* wooden hull – now well into late middle age. More modern boats would also benefit from a vibration-free environment for their electronic equipment.

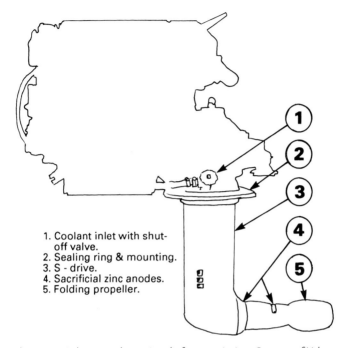

1. Coolant inlet with shut-off valve.
2. Sealing ring & mounting.
3. S - drive.
4. Sacrificial zinc anodes.
5. Folding propeller.

Fig 3.7 Volvo Penta S-drive: an alternative shaft transmission. *Courtesy of Volvo Penta.*

◆ S-DRIVES

An S-drive transmission, such as that shown in Fig 3.7, is unusual in a wooden boat, but more common in a relatively modern GRP hull that has flat sections aft between the keel and the rudder. It is also unusual for an owner to retrofit an S-drive himself, because the installation involves accurately cutting quite a large hole in the bottom of the boat and making a carefully engineered seal between the drive leg and the hull. The Volvo Penta S-drive, originally marketed as the Sail-drive, is the most well known and highly developed of this type of transmission, where the engine and drive leg form an integral unit that is flexibly mounted on a specially shaped GRP engine bed (Fig 3.8).

An S-drive makes for relatively simple installation in the sense that you have no complicated sterngear, no tricky lining up of engine and propeller shaft, and no problem of leaky sternglands. On the other hand, it is vital to make a sound job of the engine bed and of installing the flexible

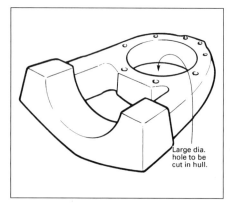

Large dia.
hole to be
cut in hull.

Fig 3.8 The Volvo GRP engine bed for mounting engine and transmission leg, which is needed when installing an S-drive. The bed itself must be bonded into the hull.

diaphragm that both seals the gap between the drive leg and the hull and isolates the drive from the hull to minimise transmitted vibration. Volvo Penta produce a special manual for the installation of their S-drives, which is worth obtaining and studying in advance if you are considering this kind of transmission.

◆ V-DRIVES

A V-drive transmission uses an angle-back gearbox so that you can install the engine 'back to front' over the propeller shaft (Fig 3.9).

The final transmission is usually through a traditional shaft and sterngear and the main advantage of a V-drive lies in the scope it allows for locating the engine further aft than would normally be the case. V-drives are more common on motor boats than sailing boats, but there can be circumstances in which their compactness might solve an installation problem where you are trying to fit a new diesel engine into an older sailing boat.

V-drives have two potential disadvantages. The first is one of accessibility, both for installation and maintenance. With the engine mounted immediately over the flexible coupling, propeller shaft and sterngland, the construction of engine bearers and the initial lining up of gearbox and shaft can be much more difficult than with a normal in-line transmission. Once the installation is complete, the sterngear is usually out of sight (and out of mind) below the engine, making it tricky to check the coupling bolts from time to time, keep an eye on the sterngland, or check the alignment should this become necessary. If you are planning to use a V-drive, it

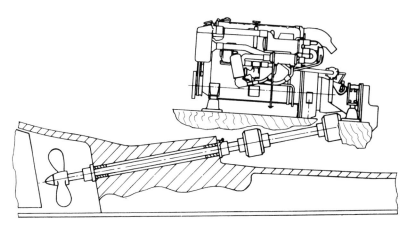

Fig 3.9 V-drive arrangement.

is worth considering fitting an Aquadrive between the gearbox and shaft so that any problems of misalignment that might otherwise develop are automatically taken care of.

The second possible snag is that because a V-drive often uses a much shorter propeller shaft than a traditional in-line transmission, there may be more difficulty in providing sufficient play in the system to accommodate the vibration of the engine on its flexible mounts. A flexible sterngland may solve the problem, or you could obtain a better engineered job by using an Aquadrive. It is worth noting that V-drive gearboxes are somewhat more expensive than standard in-line boxes, although the additional cost is not enormous if a V-drive happens to solve your installation problems neatly.

4 | Choosing the right propeller

The selection of a suitable propeller for a particular hull and engine combination is probably the most mysterious and least understood stage of installing an engine. I thought that I knew quite a lot about propellers until I started reading about how they work and talking to one or two technical experts. It then became clear to me how wide and involved the subject can be. Without plunging too deeply into propeller theory, I think it's worth examining some of the characteristics of propellers and the effect of changes in pitch, diameter and number of blades, so that one can hazard a reasonably informed choice when an expert uses his or her experience, and perhaps a computer program, to produce some propeller options for your installation.

◆ HOW A PROPELLER WORKS

Although a propeller is sometimes referred to as a screw, the simple analogy of a mechanical screw turning in a resisting medium and simply pulling itself along is not the whole story when explaining how a propeller produces thrust and drives a boat through the water. In fact, propeller blades behave more like aerofoils than the threads of a woodscrew, with their fast rotation generating relatively low water pressure on the forward faces of the blades and higher pressure on the aft faces when driving forward – and vice versa when driving astern.

For this reason, the thrust produced by a propeller cannot simply be visualised, as with the pull of a woodscrew, by the size of its 'thread' or pitch. Rather, the effective thrust derives from a more complex relationship between the pitch and profile of the blades, their length and area, the number of blades, and the revs at which the engine can turn the propeller. Engineers sometimes talk about the 'slip' of a propeller as being an inefficiency difference between the progress a boat should make in theory, reckoned by the propeller pitch times the number of revs per minute, and the distance a boat actually moves in a given time. Yet a propeller needs to slip, relative to the water in which it turns, in order to work as a pressure-generating foil, and so again it can be misleading to take the screw explanation too far.

◆ MATCHING A PROPELLER TO ENGINE AND SHAFT HORSEPOWER

When matching a propeller to a given engine installation, you face the first compromise because the marginal increase in engine or shaft horsepower starts to fall off as the engine speed is increased towards maximum rated revs, while the thrust obtained from the propeller improves as you increase revs, at something like the graph shown in Fig 4.1. You can therefore only match a propeller and engine installation at a particular rpm, ie the point at which the two graphs cross.

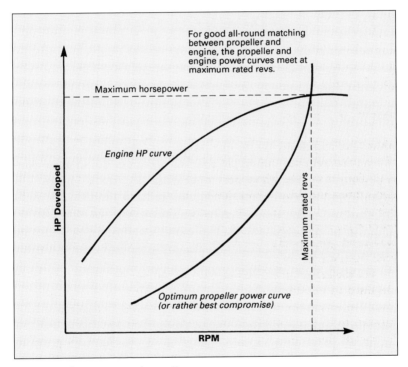

Fig 4.1 Matching engine and propeller power.

Because the engine should be free to reach or nearly reach its maximum rated revs, you really have no choice but to select a propeller that matches engine power at close to top revs. This effectively means that at speeds below maximum, the engine is able to produce more horsepower at the shaft than the propeller can absorb and convert into thrust.

Another complication is that most engines' maximum torque is delivered well below maximum rpm, sometimes at as little as 50 per cent of maximum revs for light high-speed engines. At the same time, fuel consumption per mile is usually lowest at around 70 per cent of maximum revs, while diesels suffer least wear and tear from being run fairly hard at 70–80 per cent of maximum revs. Yet again, you have to compromise. You have to choose a propeller that can use your engine's power output efficiently at around 70–85 per cent of maximum revs, but still allow the engine to reach its maximum rated speed when necessary.

◆ THE EFFECT OF DIAMETER AND PITCH

For most installations, other things being equal, the larger the propeller diameter the greater the efficiency in converting power from the engine into thrust. In fact, the diameter of a propeller is the single most significant factor in determining thrust, and a small increase in diameter greatly increases both thrust and the torque load on the engine and shaft.

Using the screw analogy, pitch is defined as the distance the propeller would pull itself along during one complete revolution, assuming it was turning in a medium in which no slip could occur. The diameter and pitch of a propeller are usually stamped on the boss with diameter given first, ie a 15 x 9 in (38 x 23 cm) propeller has a diameter of 15 in (38 cm) and a pitch of 9 in (23 cm). Increasing pitch increases propeller thrust up to a point, but a higher pitch also increases the torque load on the engine and reduces the revs at which the propeller can spin. By increasing pitch too far, you can effectively 'stall' the propeller, so that the foil sections of the blades are not able to work effectively to generate thrust.

On the basis of diameter and pitch only, therefore, one rough and ready way of choosing a propeller would be to opt for a diameter as large as you could conveniently fit into the rudder cavity or under the hull, and then select a pitch that would just provide the right torque load to allow the engine to reach its maximum rated revs at full throttle. However, you also have to consider the number and size of the propeller blades, together with the vexed question of cavitation.

◆ CAVITATION AND VENTILATION

Cavitation is a term often used rather vaguely to describe any kind of vibration or swirling noise at the propeller. In fact, cavitation is a very specific phenomenon, referring to bubbles of air at low pressure that are temporarily drawn out from the water around the propeller by excessive propeller speed or load on the blades. These low-pressure bubbles cannot survive long and they implode against the propeller causing noise, vibration and, in extreme cases, pitting of the blades. Cavitation noise can sometimes sound like a mechanical fault such as a damaged propeller or a worn stern bearing, although in many cases it is an irritation rather than a source of damage. A common cause of cavitation is too much propeller pitch, which generates a greater pressure difference between the back and front faces of the blades than can be absorbed by the passage of the boat through the water.

It is usually in relation to cavitation that you come across the terms 'blade loading' or 'blade pressure'. When engineers are working out the size and type of propeller for a particular installation, they try to keep the water pressure on the blades below a certain critical value to avoid cavitation, specifying the pitch, number of blades and the blade shape accordingly.

Ventilation, often confused with cavitation, is caused by the propeller sucking air down from the surface. It sometimes occurs in shallow draught boats where the propeller isn't sufficiently immersed in disturbance-free water. If you cannot alter the installation to overcome this, the problem is sometimes solved by fitting a slightly smaller diameter propeller than specified, so that the blades are not quite so near the surface. You can also use a propeller with blades raked slightly aft, which reduces the tendency of air to be pulled into the propeller vortex.

◆ RIGHT- OR LEFT-HANDED?

Whether you use a right- or left-handed propeller depends simply on the reduction gearbox fitted to the engine and, therefore, the final direction of rotation of the shaft. Our marginal propeller was left-handed because the old Watermota engine had a triple-chain reduction box, so the shaft rotation was in the same direction as the engine rotation. However, most gearbox outputs for single engines, including our new Perama, require a right-handed propeller.

◆ NUMBER OF BLADES

A two-bladed propeller is more efficient than a three-bladed one in the sense that, the better separated the blades, the less interfering turbulence each causes for the blade coming after it. Two-blade propellers are useful for sailing boats where you are trying to reduce drag, but ideally they need quite large diameters to give enough blade area for effective thrust, especially when going astern. A two-bladed folding propeller will reduce drag still further, although the pitch of folding propellers is often coarser than it would ideally be if you were using fixed blades. The relatively high blade loading that results can cause a degree of cavitation, which often has to be accepted as one of the costs of reducing drag.

Two-bladed propellers cause less drag, particularly when 'hidden' by the deadwood.

Where drag is not a critical consideration, three-blade propellers are generally reckoned to provide a good compromise between balance, blade area and thrust efficiency. For installations aboard larger, displacement hull boats, you could consider using a four-blade propeller if, for example, the ideal specification was for an 18 in (46 cm) diameter three-blade, but there was only the physical room to swing a diameter of 16 in (41 cm). Sufficient thrust might then be obtained from a carefully pitched 16 in (41 cm) four-blader.

◆ CHOOSING A PROPELLER

For the do-it-yourself engineer, the best way of making an informed choice about propellers is to use one of the computer programs that have been refined over the years. We called on the computer-based propeller selection

Three-bladed propellers are generally considered to provide a good compromise between balance, blade area and thrust efficiency.

service provided by Perkins, and most of the main engine manufacturers should have access to a similar facility.

Lancing Marine, the marinising engineers based near Brighton, offer a free propeller selection service using their own well developed programs, and will then supply the right propeller for the job after careful consultation. You need to supply the following information, which can be given over the phone:

- The general shape of your hull, ie whether displacement, semi-displacement or planing.
- The total laden weight including all your normal gear and equipment, stores, fuel and water, and crew.
- The waterline length.
- The number of engines.
- The engine hp and rpms at which you want to match the propeller. If in doubt about this, quote the maximum brake horsepower and maximum rated revs from the engine handbook.
- Reduction ratio of the gearbox.

From these inputs you will obtain a wealth of information, including the predicted boat speed at the quoted revs, the recommended propeller size and shape, and the torque loading for choosing the right flexible coupling. Contact Mike Bellamy or Mark Dooley at Lancing Marine on (01273) 410025.

◆ CONNECTING THE PROPELLER

Most propellers are fitted to their shaft by means of a machined taper, key and keyway, with a large securing nut on the end of the shaft, locked with a split pin, holding the propeller tight on to the taper. The end of the shaft has to be accurately machined to the same taper as the hole in the propeller boss, a job best left to propeller and shaft specialists. Most marine engineers have contacts with a local machine-shop that can turn up a propeller shaft and match the taper to that of your chosen propeller. Lancing Marine, T Norris Ltd and Vetus den Ouden Ltd are three of the better known suppliers of shafts, propellers and sterngear generally.

Precise machining of the shaft and fitting of the propeller is important not just for the security of the job, but also to achieve a near perfect balance of the propeller–shaft combination in order to minimise vibration and wear. The propeller itself must be well made and balanced, because very small imperfections can cause considerable vibration, when you consider that the shaft may be spinning at over 20 revs per second.

You may be lucky enough to be able to use your original shaft and propeller, provided you are re-engining with a unit of similar horsepower, and operating revs that gives the same direction of shaft rotation. If the new engine requires a shorter shaft than the old one, it might be feasible simply to shorten the shaft at the engine end. Or, if the shaft is worn where it passes through the cutless bearing or sterngland, it might be possible to cut off the old propeller taper, turn the shaft end for end, and machine a taper on what is now the outer end – thereby giving your shaft a new (and economical) lease of life.

◆ LUBRICATION

We retained the original sterngland greaser, with its large brass reservoir mounted near the cockpit for easy access. Grease is forced down a flexible pipe and into the sterntube at the sterngland bearing, just abaft the packing box. Thus the packing string itself is lubricated, but most of the increase is pushed back along the sterntube to lubricate the shaft, emerging as a watery mixture to lubricate the cutless bearing.

Stormalong in the Nash Holden dry dock barge at Old Mill Boatyard, Dartmouth. In practice, the 15 in (38 cm) x 9 in (23 cm) three-bladed prop has proved about right.

◆ SACRIFICIAL ANODE

The zinc sacrificial anode mounted on the outside of the hull is wired to the engine and the sterntube. I'll be looking at the fitting and wiring of anodes in Chapter 7.

◆ EVALUATION

Our 15 in (38 cm) x 9 in (23 cm) three-bladed propeller seems about right. The size recommended by Perkins was 15 in (38 cm) x 8½ in (21 cm) for matching at maximum rated revs, and I added the extra 12 mm (½ in) of pitch with their approval for a shade more 'bite' when manoeuvring and going astern, and also because we would normally be running at about 2500 revs. The propeller generates a bit of noise at this cruising speed – a type of rapid clicking that doesn't really sound like cavitation. I suspect this is water pressure noise caused by the proximity of the middle rudder pintle to the top of the propeller. As a general rule, you should have clearance of at least 15 per cent of the propeller diameter between the blade tips and any part of the hull, ie about 2¼ in (5.7 cm) for our 15 in (38 cm) propeller. The pintle is rather closer than this, but there is no easy way of increasing the clearance except using a smaller-diameter propeller, which I am reluctant to do. There does not appear to be any problem of increased propeller wear, so we will probably leave well alone.

A valuable reference on the subject of choosing the right propeller is *The Propeller Handbook* by Dave Gerr (published by International Marine/ Ragged Mountain Press International). This is a mine of information for anyone contemplating their own engine installation.

Engine electrics and | 5
charging

In one sense, it seems natural enough to regard engine electrics, engine controls and instruments as auxiliary equipment that may well be specified and fitted at quite a late stage in a new installation. On the other hand, it is important that these aspects are given enough thought early on, so that you don't box yourself into a corner, quite literally, on the question of cable runs or the location of batteries, switches, engine instruments or gear and throttle controls. You also need to budget for this 'auxiliary' side of things, since the cost of a workmanlike battery set-up and good quality engine controls can be rather more than auxiliary, steadily totting its way up to a significant sum.

Stormalong's basic electrical supply would remain more or less unchanged under the new diesel engine regime, with two heavy-duty largish capacity 12V batteries secured in their dry, airy compartment under the after deck. However, we wanted to renew most of the wiring, improve the switching, and at least think about one or two sophistications to the charging system. On the engine controls and instruments front there were going to be quite a few innovations, and I will be looking at the various options we considered in Chapter 6.

◆ BATTERY CAPACITY

One of the falsest economies aboard a boat, whether sail or power, is to fit batteries of dubious quality or too low a capacity. Since very few modern marine engines can be swung by hand, a reliable starting battery is of vital importance. You need to bear in mind that the high compression ratio of a diesel, and the need to build up heat quickly in the cylinders, mean that the engine has to be cranked at a brisk speed for efficient starting. For this, a well-charged battery is a must. Only fairly small dayboats ought to rely on a single battery to provide power for both engine starting and for basic auxiliaries such as cabin and navigation lights. A double battery installation should be standard for any boat that ventures offshore at night.

However, there are various schools of thought about how battery capacity should be divided between engine starting and general 'services'.

Some owners prefer to fit a heavy-duty, high-capacity services battery which is designed to cope with a considerable discharge before recharging (often referred to as 'deep cycling'), and then have a starting battery of moderate capacity, but designed specifically to produce a heavy discharge current for a short time, be topped up quickly once the engine starts, and then remain happily inactive for a longish period of time until called upon to start the engine again.

My own preference, on the other hand, is to have two identical high-capacity batteries, which I can alternate while cruising using the changeover switch, so that each battery serves a turn for engine starting and services. While powering the services, the 'battery of the week' benefits from regular charging and discharging, which is good for the battery plates and the general condition of the cells. Meanwhile, the battery on engine duty has a chance to become as nearly fully charged as the regulator will allow, gradually being topped up as the engine is run each day. The only disadvantage with this system is that you have to keep track of which battery is being used for which job, and make sure that the engine battery is always given enough charging but is switched out whenever the engine is stopped.

In fact, *Stormalong* has two 12V tractor batteries, each of 100 ampere-hours (Ah) capacity. In theory, a 100 Ah battery is one that from full charge can deliver 1 A of current for 100 hours, 5 A for 20 hours, 10 A for 10 hours, and so on. In practice, a battery can rarely be charged to its maximum capacity, and the current it delivers will fall off progressively during discharge. The faster a battery is discharged, the less its theoretical capacity can be used effectively, and so capacity is always quoted for a particular discharge period – usually 10 hours but sometimes (with larger batteries) for 20 hours.

Most ordinary car batteries, typically rated at 40 Ah or 50 Ah, have too limited a capacity for marine use, especially where engines are run only infrequently. You need to allow some reserve for the self-discharge that occurs when a battery stands idle for long periods. This natural discharge can be 12–13 per cent of capacity per month for conventional car batteries, although it is usually much less (perhaps 4–5 per cent) for specialised marine batteries. You can, of course, connect batteries together *in parallel* to increase capacity (as in Fig 5.1) – eg two 50 Ah batteries in parallel give you a nominal total of 100 Ah.

Different types of lead-acid batteries have different discharge characteristics. Some batteries, those with thinner but multiple plates, are best

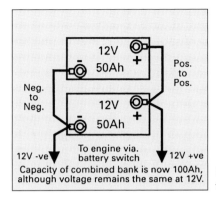

Capacity of combined bank is now 100Ah, although voltage remains the same at 12V.

Fig 5.1 Connecting batteries in parallel to increase capacity.

suited to producing the high instantaneous current necessary for starting a diesel engine; these are often sold as starting batteries. Traction batteries, on the other hand, have a lower current potential, but are better able to sustain high discharge rates. Maintenance-free batteries, such as the gel-types supplied by Vetus and the Delco Freedom batteries supplied by Deltec Power Distributors, provide a good general-purpose compromise and perform well under most conditions, with the added advantage of minimal voltage decay when the batteries are left unused.

◆ REVIEWING YOUR BATTERY CONSUMPTION

By modern standards, *Stormalong's* batteries only have to cope with a modest line-up of electrical facilities. The main cabin lighting comes from 8 W fluorescent tubes, which only draw a miserly 0.67 A each. Three of these left on continuously for eight hours in an evening will deplete the services battery by a total of 16 Ah.

The two 25 W bunk reading lamps need watching, and the 25 W tri-colour is often left on for 10 hours during a night passage, consuming a hefty 21 Ah. The compass light takes almost nothing and the 15 W deck-light and 80 W searchlight are only used occasionally. The chart-table light takes 5 W intermittently, and we have two red night lights of 3 W each at floor level in the saloon and forepeak.

Apart from these lights, we have only the echo-sounder and a radio/cassette player running off the ship's supply. *Stormalong* seems to cruise happily enough without a VHF, an electric bilge pump or anchor winch, a fridge or a GPS. The fresh-water system is manual and our anchor light will burn for a night, a day and another night on a cupful of paraffin.

When trying to estimate your required battery capacity, it can be salutary to carry out a thorough electrical audit, listing every item of electrical equipment on board, together with its power consumption when switched on and the actual charge likely to be taken from the battery during a typical period of use. Some equipment takes quite a high burst of power when running, but is never used for very long at any one time.

Electric anchor winches come into this category. For example, a medium-sized foredeck winch might well be taking 30 A of current when hauling steadily under load. Usually, of course, the engine will be running when you are operating an electric winch, but in any case, with luck, the winch should not be on for more than two or three minutes and you therefore would not drain the battery by more than about 1½ Ah even with the engine off. Similarly, a powerful searchlight might take up to 10 A of current when switched on, but in practice will only be used for a few seconds at a time.

A VHF radio draws considerably more current on 'transmit' (perhaps up to 4 A when broadcasting at 25 W) than on 'standby', when the drain is typically well under ½ A. However, when a VHF is left on standby for a long period of time, that ½ A starts to add up to significant battery usage.

In fact, once you start leaving items of equipment running as a matter of course, a creeping build-up of apparently small consumptions can start to accumulate into a serious power loss. The Decca does not use much current, you might think, maybe 0.25 A for an average size of set; and a fridge only takes about 1 A when it is right down to temperature and you don't open the door too often. If, though, a 90 Ah service battery is only 70 per cent charged at the start of a day's sailing – a common enough state of affairs – this leaves you with a maximum of 63 Ah to play with. Half an amp for the VHF on standby, ¼ A for the GPS, 1 A for the fridge, and a bit for the fresh-water pressure pump now and again, might give you 2 A of steady drain during a typical sailing day.

Ten hours of this treatment takes your 'heavy-duty' battery down to 43 Ah, which is under half the nominal capacity. It might then get a short burst of charging as you motor into your berth or anchorage, but then the poor thing is expected to cope with an evening of lights, music, and the fresh-water pump working overtime as members of the crew cook, wash up and clean their teeth.

Having worked out a few sums along these lines, one can be alarmed into the habit of keeping things switched off unless absolutely necessary. In practice, when trying to decide on an appropriate size of service battery, a useful rule of thumb is to work out a generous daily electrical consumption in ampere-hours, and then multiply this by three to give a minimum battery capacity to support this usage. If, for example, all your lights and equipment could easily consume 40 Ah over a 24-hour period, your service battery ought to be at least 120 Ah capacity. If in doubt, err on the side of overkill for battery size, especially if your alternator is fitted with a standard voltage regulator – which almost certainly won't be using your charging capability to full advantage.

At the same time, your alternator has to be powerful enough to support whatever battery capacity you decide on. Another handy rule is that your steady-state charging current – ie the current going in once the battery has taken an initial heavy charge, built up a counter voltage and settled down – ought to be somewhere between 10–15 per cent of total capacity. By this reckoning, the steady-state charging rate for 120 Ah of battery capacity should be 12–18 A. To give your alternator a safe working load, the upper limit of this steady rate should not exceed two-thirds of the alternator's rated output, ie a 28 A alternator would just about be sufficient to support one 120 Ah battery.

The alternator on our Perkins Perama is rated at 55 A, so by the two-thirds rule it should be large enough to provide 36 A of continuous steady charging. Then, following the 10–15 per cent rule, it looks as though this working charge rate could support $36 \div 15\% = 240$ Ah of capacity – two batteries of 120 Ah each, say, one for starting and one for services. If possible, it is preferable to stay well within the two-thirds rule. While most engine manufacturers claim that their alternators have a continuous rating at the nominal amperage, it is also the case that most alternators were originally designed for automotive rather than marine use. In practice, alternators usually get much hotter in the confined engine compartment of a boat than under a car bonnet, so they have a harder life as a result.

Several engine manufacturers now offer the option of larger alternators to cope with increasing power requirements aboard most cruising boats. For their BD1005 28 hp diesel, for example, Beta Marine can supply a 100 amp alternator in place of their standard 65 amp and Yanmar offer an 80 amp for their 3YM30 engine instead of the standard 60 amp. Volvo Penta have moved even further with their D1-30 engine, which has a 115 amp alternator as standard. This 14 volt alternator has an electronic charging regulator and delivers a good 35 amps at idling speed and about 100 amps at normal cruising speed.

In an interesting development, Beta Marine can now supply a 230-volt mains generator powered by its own belt from their engine's front end PTO pulley. Available in either 3,5 kVA or 7 kVA versions, this Beta Marine 'Travel Power' system produces a stable 230-volt single-phase mains supply at any engine speed, regulated through a power control box.

◆ SITING BATTERIES

There are several factors to bear in mind when deciding where to site batteries. First and foremost, batteries need to be securely strapped down in a dry location, preferably in their own acid-proof boxes; there should be no risk of them shifting or being dowsed with sea water in heavy weather. Batteries should be covered, so that you cannot drop spanners on to them and cause an accidental short. Good ventilation to the outside is important, since lead-acid cells give off a certain amount of potentially explosive hydrogen gas when being charged.

Weight can be significant, since a pair of heavy-duty batteries might weigh upwards of 68 kg (150 lb); *Stormalong's* batteries are not in the best place from this point of view, being right aft, but they are well protected and ventilated, and tucked out of the way. On the other hand, easy access is desirable, however 'maintenance-free' your batteries claim to be. Even with sealed batteries, which never need topping up with distilled water, you should check the terminals from time to time for tightness and corrosion. Finally, while taking account of these various factors, try to install batteries as near the engine as possible, to avoid long cable runs and the associated voltage drop.

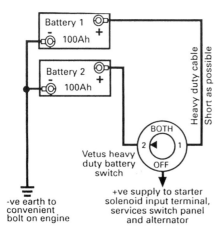

Fig 5.2 Battery switching circuit.

◆ BATTERY SWITCHING

Stormalong's two batteries are wired through a Vetus heavy-duty changeover switch, as shown in Fig 5.2. This enables switching between either or both batteries while the engine is running. This last point is important because an alternator will quickly be damaged by charging an open circuit, ie with the battery switched off or disconnected. It is well worth protecting your alternator with a surge-diode device, which will detect the rapidly rising voltage if an alternator is open-circuited and then switch the charging output safely to earth.

The arrangement in Fig 5.2 means that with the changeover switch at position 1, the engine will charge battery 1 when running, and both the services and starter motor will draw from battery 1 when they are used. The same reasoning applies for the 'battery 2' and 'both' positions. The battery management system, if you like, is completely manual, in that the changeover switch dictates which battery is being charged and used.

This is probably the most common set-up aboard sailing boats and has the advantage of simplicity, although you have to keep track of which battery is well up or well down, and remember to switch to the engine battery before starting the engine and switch back to the services battery after the engine has been charging for a while.

More sophisticated arrangements are possible, one being that the starter motor always draws from its own battery, the services from their own battery, and the charging circuit is wired to charge both batteries whenever the engine is running. This will involve fitting a blocking diode

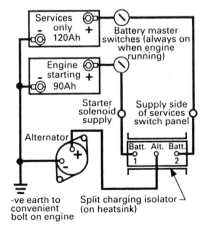

Fig 5.3 Wiring a split charging battery isolator.

or 'battery isolator' in the battery circuit; this allows the alternator to charge both batteries together, but prevents current flowing from the most well-charged battery – normally the starting battery – to the least-charged when the engine is stopped.

Fig 5.3 shows how an isolator can be wired. One disadvantage of this system is that the blocking diode in the isolator actually consumes quite a bit of current, which may be significant aboard a sailing boat where the engine is used infrequently for short periods. This 'wasted' power is converted into heat that has to be dissipated, so the isolator should really be mounted in a well-ventilated spot outside the engine compartment. Battery isolators can be quite expensive – I priced a suitable unit at nearly £70 when we were reviewing *Stormalong*'s battery arrangements.

◆ CHARGE CONTROL

Alternators control their output voltage according to the state of charge of the battery. The more a battery is charged, the higher its voltage becomes and so the alternator voltage must also rise to keep pushing current into the battery. When the battery is fully charged, however, the alternator voltage has to be prevented from rising further so that charging will stop. These are the basic functions of the regulator.

For regulation to be possible, of course, the alternator must somehow assess the battery voltage as charging takes place. Most alternators are 'machine-sensed', ie their regulator measures the charging voltage as it leaves the alternator. The regulator then rapidly switches the alternator field coil on and off at a rate that keeps the charging voltage sufficiently higher than the battery voltage for a net charging current to flow. This charging voltage is nominally 14 V for a 12 V battery.

A marked inefficiency of this system aboard boats is that the regulator has no idea of the sometimes considerable voltage drop in the cables and switches between alternator and battery. The actual voltage received by the battery will be lower than the voltage sensed by the regulator. Ideally, a correspondingly 'higher than normal' alternator voltage is needed if enough charging current is to flow into the battery.

It is better to have a 'battery-sensing' regulator, which measures the charging voltage arriving at the battery terminals and increases the alternator voltage needed to overcome any drop and produce an effective charging current. Various companies now supply special battery-sensing and charge control systems that can be retrofitted to machine-sensed alternators.

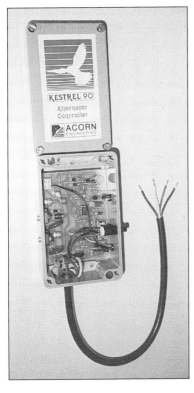

The Kestrel 90 Alternator Controller, a good value battery-sensing regulator which has four connections and is easy to install.

Three of the most well known are the Kestrel 90 Alternator Controller, made in the UK by Acorn Engineering; the Swedish TWC Mark II Advanced Regulator, distributed in the UK by Aqua-Marine; and the ADVERC Battery Management System, developed from the TWC system by Trevor Scarratt and made in the UK by Adverc BM Ltd.

The Kestrel 90 is the simplest, least expensive and most easily fitted, offering two important advantages over basic machine-sensing. The first is a facility to keep the charging current constant, instead of the charge rate falling away as charging progresses. This reduces the charging time and is an obvious benefit where an auxiliary engine is only infrequently used.

The second facility is an automatic boost to the charging voltage, which is triggered when the engine is started and cuts out after a pre-programmed period. This boost quickly replaces power to a heavily discharged battery, such as the services battery after a night's use, and allows charging much closer to a battery's maximum capacity than you can achieve with simple machine-sensing. A practical point in favour of the Kestrel is that no modification is required to the alternator itself.

The TWC and ADVERC systems also use battery-sensing regulators, but incorporate more sophisticated charging programmes than the one-off boost provided by the Kestrel 90. The ADVERC and TWC Mark II give a tightly controlled charging programme with 'rest' periods after every four charging cycles of twenty minutes. Both are robustly cased and well designed for marine use. Installation of either system is generally rather more involved than for the Kestrel, since the TWC or ADVERC usually replace the existing regulator while the Kestrel operates in parallel to it. Where the original regulator is effectively part of the alternator, you may need to buy a replacement brush-holder or conversion kit when fitting a TWC or ADVERC.

These add-on regulator systems are not exactly inexpensive, but are worth considering if you often find your services battery well down while the battery itself is of adequate capacity and in good condition. It is in fact quite common for boats with plenty of electrical equipment on board, but limited engine running time, to have service batteries that are only 60–70 per cent charged for most of their lives. This means in practice that only about 30 per cent of total battery capacity is ever available for useful work, and also leads to premature battery deterioration from sulphation of the plates.

In the event, I didn't install one of these charge control systems, partly because our battery capacity is generous for *Stormalong*'s requirements and we had never had trouble with low batteries in the past, but partly because the original engine budget was already groaning at the seams. However, I am convinced by most of the arguments for more effective charge control on marine engines, and may well add one of these systems in the future.

Lucas A127 alternator. The arrow shows where to make the 'Field' connection (the green wire) from the Kestrel Controller.

◆ WIRING THE ENGINE TO THE BATTERY

You would think, perhaps, that this would be a perfectly simple operation. There you are with the battery system organised, with its changeover switch and any other sophistications all neatly wired in. There stands the new engine, just waiting to have the positive feed and negative earth cable connected to it. Surely it is just a matter of spannering a couple of heavy duty spade terminals on to a pair of wiring posts, positive to positive, negative to negative?

Well, not exactly, since most engine manufacturers seem to make life a bit more complicated at this point. Perkins were no exception and the physical access to the critical terminal at the back of the starter solenoid really needed the attention of a dwarf engineer with extra short arms and 10-inch fingers with double joints.

It would be too easy, I suppose, to have two clearly marked wiring posts somewhere accessible on the engine – one to take the positive cable from the battery supply, and the other, leading to earth, to take the negative cable. The question probably doesn't get asked very often, since most engines are installed and wired by engineers who instinctively know their way around.

The earth connection is usually no problem. You just need to choose a suitable stud or bolt around the engine, preferably one attaching some auxiliary piece of equipment. I used the fuel filter bracket, cleaning the underside of the bolt head with emery paper to make a good electrical

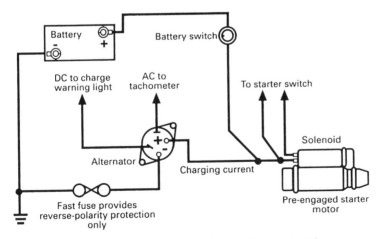

Fig 5.4 Basic wiring between battery, alternator and starter/solenoid.

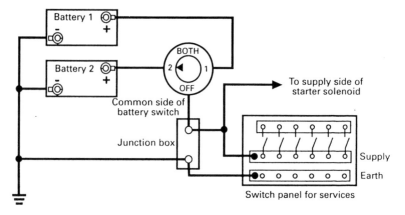

Fig 5.5 Wiring-in the services panel.

contact and tightening it back on to the engine with a large spade terminal underneath.

For most negative earth engines, the battery positive cable should lead either straight or indirectly to the supply side of the starter motor solenoid. When the starter key is turned to the 'crank' position, the electromagnetic switch in the solenoid is made and battery current is fed through to the supply side of the starter motor (see the wiring diagram in Fig 5.4).

◆ SUPPLYING THE SERVICES

With the batteries safely connected to the engine, there remains the question of how best to wire your electrical equipment into this power supply. *Stormalong's* battery switching system is shown in Fig 5.2 – all battery power is tapped off for auxiliaries *after* it has passed the main selector switch. Therefore, switching the batteries off switches everything off; switching to 'both' means that power is drawn from both batteries and the engine charges both; switching to 'battery one' means that all power is drawn from battery one and only battery one is charged – and similarly for battery two.

Fig 5.5 shows how the power supply is wired from the *common* side of the battery selector to a Vetus six-way panel, which has a monitoring LED and tubular glass fuse for each function switch. We could have used a more expensive panel equipped with circuit breakers instead of fuses, but there is nothing wrong with straightforward fuses so long as you keep enough spares on board. Since *Stormalong's* electrical equipment is all quite basic, there was no need to supply certain auxiliaries from one battery rather than another. However, there can be advantages, for example, in wiring a GPS set to a dedicated services battery such as that shown in Fig 5.3. Then your navigation equipment will never be confused by the heavy voltage drop that occurs when the starter motor is switched in.

By the same token, it might be advantageous to wire an electric anchor winch, which takes a high current for a short time, to a dedicated *engine starting* battery, again to prevent a sharp voltage drop from resetting your navigation equipment. In most cases, the engine would be running while the anchor winch was being used, so there would be no real risk of draining the starting battery. Fig 5.6 shows how to separate the supply of certain auxiliaries in this way.

An invaluable book covering marine electrics is *Boatowner's Mechanical and Electrical Manual* by Nigel Calder (Adlard Coles Nautical).

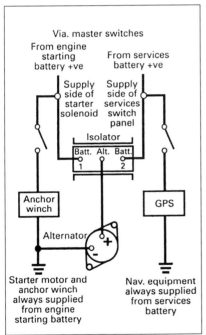

Fig 5.6 Supplying certain auxiliaries from different batteries.

6 | Controls and instruments

When you buy a boat, either new or secondhand, in which the engine works perfectly well in all respects, the question of controls and instruments probably never arises. They are fitted, they work, and that's all there is to it. Only when installing an engine yourself do you become aware of the intricacies and the cost of various control mechanisms and the importance of choosing the right equipment for the job.

Stormalong's old engine had acquired a distinctly Heath Robinson throttle arrangement, using a historic brass control and a length of bowden cable linked to numerous springs and levers. We had always intended to improve this set-up, but never quite got around to it. The throttle used to stick at inconvenient moments, often lingering at 'half ahead' long after you'd tried to select 'dead slow'. Then it might close suddenly and cut out the engine, leaving you gliding towards a quay with no means of stopping.

The gearshift was also somewhat eccentric. You had to remove a small panel in the cockpit sole and feel around with your foot – a system that confounded most helmsmen, but involved even skilled operators in a frantic series of curtsies when manoeuvring in tight corners. I would often covet a slick, single-lever control when we were backing and filling in a fresh breeze, with our long bowsprit swinging a perilous arc around a crowded marina.

◆ GEAR AND THROTTLE CONTROLS

There is an amazingly wide range of marine engine controls on the market, from specialist control manufacturers such as Morse and Kobelt, from the larger engine manufacturers, and from general equipment suppliers such as Vetus. Apart from the basic manual controls that use push–pull cables, more sophisticated electric, hydraulic, pneumatic and wire-over-pulley systems are available for larger engines. The Morse SLE electronic controls have become popular aboard cruising motorboats. However, our new Perkins Perama was designed to be fitted with standard manual Morse controls and Red Jaket cables, which together provide a very smooth gearshift so long as everything is carefully installed, the control head is firmly mounted, and the cable turns are not too tight.

The Perama's Hurth HBW50 gearbox needs only a modest push–pull force to operate its gear lever through the required 35 mm (just under 1½ in) in either direction. Although the shift is not activated by an oil pump, as with the Borg Warner hydraulic gearboxes, the Hurth does have a servo action once minimal pressure is brought to bear on the forward or reverse clutches. This initial frictional contact causes a disc carrier to spin on the output shaft, a clever centrifugal device that then sets the gear engagement in train. The throttle, of course, requires only a light push–pull force, moving through about 40 mm (just over 1½ in) at the engine from idle to fully open.

◆ CHOOSING A CONTROL HEAD

Most sailing boats need a side-mounted unit with the 'works' protected behind a bulkhead or cockpit coaming. A single-lever control is usually preferable to having separate levers for throttle and gearshift. Top-mounted controls are used mainly in motorboats, at the wheelhouse console or up on a flying bridge. Some factors to consider when choosing a control are: (i) quality of engineering; (ii) size, especially that part of the mechanism behind the scenes; (iii) weatherproofing; (iv) style; (v) price.

Quality of engineering
To some extent, as with most boat equipment, you get what you pay for. The more expensive the control unit, the better made and smoother to operate it tends to be. However, you can't go far wrong with the least expensive controls from any of the well known names. All Morse controls, for example, are well designed and put together even at the 'budget' end of the range, as are the popular controls supplied by Volvo Penta and Vetus.

Size
Stormalong's cockpit is quite small, so we were looking for as compact a unit as possible. One of the popular Morse controls, the long-running MV2, was a likely contender from this point of view. It needed a panel cutout of only 110 mm x 90 mm (about 4¼ in x 3½ in) and is clear space of 282 mm x 90 mm x 60 mm (11¼ in x 3½ in x 2½ in) behind the panel. A more modern-looking alternative to the MV2 is the new SL3 control, which was launched recently at the Earls Court Boat Show.

Another option when I was searching the market were the well designed Vetus side-mounted controls, of which the stainless steel Sisco model is smart and workmanlike.

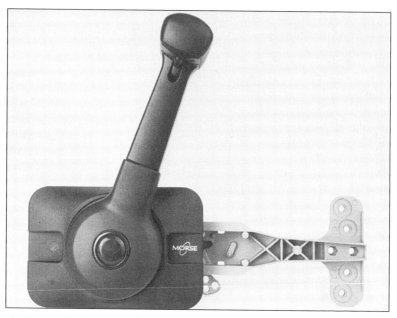

The Morse SL3 side-mounted control is a stylish successor to the popular MV2 and would sit well in most modern cockpits. *Courtesy: Morse Controls Ltd.*

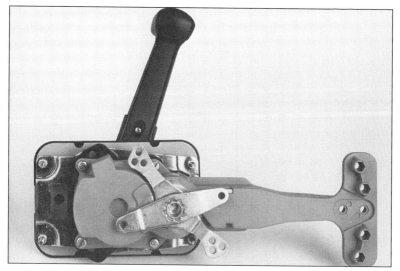

The business end of the Morse SL3 side-mounted control which works on a different principle to the popular MV2. It represents good value for money. *Courtesy: Morse Controls Ltd.*

Weatherproofing

Strange as it may seem, marine engine controls vary considerably in their ability to stand up to the harsh conditions of a sailboat cockpit. Morse MV2 controls, for example, are often mounted outside, but I have seen quite a few whose chrome control levers are badly corroded and pitted. It was also interesting that the KL control was described somewhat cautiously in the catalogue as: '. . . ideal for exposed installations, being designed to splash-proof standards . . .'. 'Splash-proof' sounded a bit feeble, and I thought of the heavy green water that can break into the cockpit during a fresh blow in mid-Channel. It is not so much the water itself that causes problems, but the salty deposits left behind when a control unit has had a good soaking and eventually dries out. Like most equipment on a boat, however heavy duty it is claimed to be, a control unit will need regular preventative maintenance – even if this is only a generous squirt of WD40 from time to time.

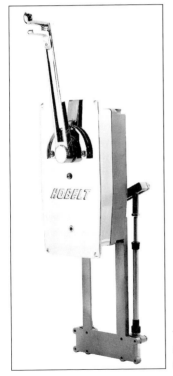

This smart and practical Volvo Penta PC-741 engine control is fitted with a sailboat lever. This well-made unit has a timeless design.

If you have plenty of mounting space, some of the most robust controls I have seen are made by the Canadian company Kobelt and distributed in the UK by Wagner Engineering. They are on the pricey side, but are extremely well engineered in die-cast brass and stainless steel. The Kobelt 2044-KW is a good side-mounted control suitable for sailing boats.

Style

Because *Stormalong* is a traditional wooden boat, we didn't want the control unit to look too flashy. The Morse MV2 scored well with its simple understated design, but some of the controls we looked at were pretty garish and would have been out of place aboard a 1936 gaff cutter. At the same time, either the MV2, the timeless styling of the Morse SL3, or the well known Volvo Penta PC-741 sit well in most modern cockpits.

If you can afford them, many of the Kobelt controls have a clean functional elegance that makes them ideal for traditional boats. Although their more substantial controls could only be fitted in quite large boats, the Kobelt top-mounted units with brass finish would look well in the wheelhouse of a classic motor yacht.

◆ STOP CONTROL

A diesel engine can have two types of stop control. The most common is a straightforward manual control whereby a lever in the cockpit or wheelhouse is linked by a single push–pull cable to the shut-off lever at the fuel injection pump. You simply pull the control to stop the engine, push it back into place when the engine has stopped, and then switch off the starter key at the instrument panel. With this set-up, you will need to find somewhere convenient to mount the control, which also gives a clear cable run down to the engine.

The simplest type of manual stop control uses a 'T' handle screwed to the end of a push–pull cable, which is then mounted through a convenient bulkhead or on to the instrument panel. There are also various fittings that allow the 'T' handle to be side-mounted at an angle (see Fig 6.1), eg the Morse model DC in stainless steel and the cheaper Vetus Type DC in black plastic.

A more sophisticated system uses an engine-mounted solenoid to pull the fuel shut-off lever. The solenoid can either be operated by a separate push button on the instrument panel, which I think is the best arrangement; or, on some engines, by pushing the starter key in, turning it all the way to the left, and holding it there until the engine stops and you can switch the key off.

◆ CHOOSING THE CABLES

You should always use the correct type of push–pull cable for whichever control unit you finally choose. The most commonly used aboard yachts is the Morse Type 33C 'Red Jaket' cable, which is supplied in any length to the nearest quarter of a metre. Volvo Penta supply an equivalent Type 333, also to the nearest quarter of a metre, and Vetus do a Type 33 to the nearest foot. Don't try to economise or improvise by using automotive cable or heavy-duty bowden cable – it won't last long on a boat, the controls almost certainly won't work smoothly, and you risk damaging an expensive gearbox through incorrect travel of the gearshift lever.

The Type 33 Morse cables, and their equivalent from Volvo Penta and Vetus, are robustly made with tough sheathing, seals and a swivel at each end, and a low-friction conduit (see Fig 6.2). However, it is important not to have tight turns in the cable run between the control unit and engine.

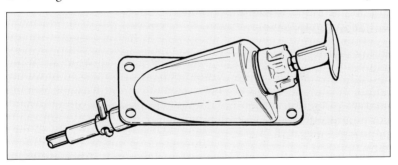

Fig 6.1 Diesel stop control.

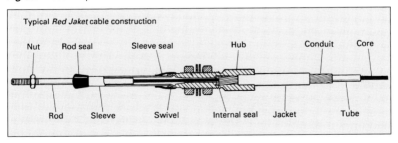

Fig 6.2 Construction of Morse type engine control cables.

For installations where tight turns seem to be unavoidable, Keypart of Watford supply a Morse-compatible push–pull cable known as 'Keyflex', which is more flexible than the standard Morse or Vetus Type 33 and can be successfully run along quite tortuous routes.

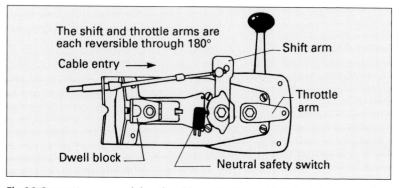

Fig 6.3 Connecting gear and throttle cables to the Morse MV2 single-lever control.

◆ INSTALLING THE CONTROL AND CABLES

To anyone with a sympathy for things mechanical, a single-lever control head is an intriguing piece of engineering. The principle is simple but clever, as shown in the diagram of the Morse MV2 (see Fig 6.3). The shift arm can be reversed through 180 degrees depending on which way round you install the control and whether the engine needs a push or a pull action to engage ahead. The throttle arm can also be reversed, depending on whether a push or pull action is required to open the throttle. Both the shift and throttle arms, especially the latter, depend on the cable being able to swivel freely from where it enters the control unit – which is one reason why it is important to use the correct Morse or compatible cable. You will also find that the Morse cable terminals are exactly the right length and type for most engine control units.

Moving the MV2 control lever away from neutral starts the gear cable moving straightaway, but the first movement of the throttle arm simply allows a spring in the dwell block to decompress. This means that while the engine is being shifted from neutral to ahead or astern, the moving throttle arm in the control head should have no effect on the throttle cable and the engine should stay at idling speed. When connecting the throttle cable to the throttle arm in the control unit, you therefore need to adjust the terminal position carefully so that the engine only starts to accelerate once ahead or astern gear has been fully engaged.

Coupling the cables to the engine also requires careful adjustment. For the gearshift, you first need to make sure that the shift lever on the engine is *exactly* in neutral (usually dead upright) when the control lever is clicked into its neutral position. This involves accurately locating the connecting terminal along its thread at the cable end. Then it is important that the shift lever on the engine is given exactly the right amount of travel between neutral and ahead, and between neutral and astern. There are normally two or three alternative fixing points on the engine shift lever to get this right (see Fig 6.4).

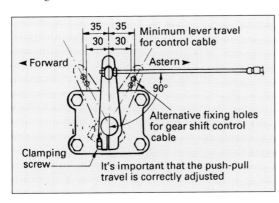

Fig 6.4 Gearbox cable connections.

For our Hurth HBW50 gearbox, for example, the cable travel should be at least 35 mm (just under 1½ in) from neutral to ahead or neutral to astern when the terminal is connected to the top hole in the gearbox shift lever. The travel can exceed 35 mm by a little, because the shift lever just floats once the gear has been engaged, but having slightly less than 35 mm push or pull will over time cause clutch wear and possibly gearbox damage.

Having carefully set up the throttle and gearshift cables during the installation, you need to check from time to time that everything is working smoothly and, in particular, to ensure that: (a) the engine speed always stays at idle until ahead or astern is fully engaged, and (b) the gearbox shift lever is always given the correct amount of travel.

◆ ENGINE INSTRUMENTS

Most new engines are supplied with a basic instrument panel, complete with a wiring harness and multi-plug to make a foolproof connection between the panel and the engine. The standard harness for the Perama was 4 m (13 ft) long, which was plenty for the short distance between the engine compartment and our chosen spot in the cockpit for the instruments.

Few instrument panels for marine engines are as weatherproof as they should be, so you should try to install them in as protected a location as possible – out of the direct line of fire of heavy dollops of sea water. The wiring harness and multi-plug should also be kept dry as far as possible. We wrapped the multi-plug in several layers of insulating tape once it was securely connected, and the harness was clipped so that it couldn't snag into wet bilges or hang too close to the hottest parts of the engine.

The Perama's basic instruments are a fresh-water temperature gauge and a tachometer (rev counter), with warning lights for oil pressure and charging. I was happy enough with an oil pressure light, but would like to have had an ammeter instead of the alternator light. It is always reassuring to see how much current is going into (or out of) the batteries, and the charging rate does give you some idea of the state of each battery.

I consider the temperature gauge to be valuable, because it can give you early warning about, for example, a faulty thermostat or a partial blockage of the water inlet by weed or a plastic bag. In fact, quite a small change in the rate of sea-water flow will show up as a change in fresh-water temperature, so this gauge can be a surprisingly sensitive diagnostic device.

A tachometer is definitely worth its place on the instrument panel, and I would have installed one had it not been part of the basic kit. For a start, it is handy to be able to check and adjust the idling speed as soon as the engine is installed and running, and periodically thereafter. Also, when the engine is run in, you can assess how well the propeller is matched to the engine and hull by seeing how close you can get to the maximum rated revs.

When motoring for long periods on passage, you want to be running at a cruising speed such that the engine is working hard enough for its own good, but also giving reasonably economical fuel consumption. A tachometer helps you set the right revs for this compromise, especially if you know something about the engine's power output graph. A tacho-meter is useful for crews on watch, who can slow down to avoid ships or negotiate crabpots, but then come back to the right cruising revs once the diversion is over. Bear in mind, though, that most tachometers work by measuring the frequency of the alternator AC output, which is directly proportional to engine speed. If your alternator belt is slipping at all, the tachometer will underread the engine revs.

◆ VOLTMETERS

Another instrument that can be worth fitting is a battery voltmeter, specialised versions of which are sold as 'battery state indicators' or 'circuit monitors'. Of course a voltmeter can only measure actual battery voltage if the engine is stopped and, ideally, if no auxiliary equipment is drawing current. A simple analogue (moving needle) voltmeter can be useful on board, such as those with 'low' (red) and 'OK' (green) sectors supplied by VDO or Vetus. However, the calibration of these meters is necessarily rather coarse, and quite a small movement of the needle can represent a significant change in battery voltage.

A battery state voltmeter with its red-green-red sectors to indicate low charge, OK and over-charging conditions.

For example, a fully charged battery might show a voltage of 12.6V or more, a 75 per cent charged battery perhaps 12.4V. A totally flat battery might give anything between 10.5V and 11.7V. So the difference between a fully and half-charged battery could be only 0.4V, with possibly just 0.9V between full charge and full discharge. For this reason, it is best to use a digital meter for battery monitoring, which can show the voltage to two decimal places and give a more accurate picture of the state of charge.

A sophisticated system is the multi-channel circuit monitor supplied by Adverc BM Ltd. The Adverc DCM MkIII can measure voltage and current in four separate circuits and incorporates alarms for low voltage, so that you get advance warning of excessive battery drain.

◆ ENGINE HOUR METERS

An engine hour meter simply clocks up the total number of hours running to give some guidance on the frequency of oil changes and servicing. In fact, an hour meter is not really necessary for most yachts, provided that you follow the time periods in the engine manufacturer's maintenance schedule. Most important is to have a regular routine for changing the engine oil at the beginning and end of each season, changing the gearbox oil at least every 12 months, draining off and cleaning the fuel pre-filter and water separator every two or three months, and renewing fuel cartridge filters at least every 12 months. I would probably only consider installing an hour meter where an engine has a much greater than average use – aboard a charter or sailing school boat, for example.

◆ FUEL GAUGES

I am not a great fan of fuel gauges on boats, having come across many that are inaccurate or only work intermittently. A sight gauge is much better if you can organise one – there's nothing to go wrong and you can actually see the fuel level for yourself. Alternatively, why not simply use a carefully calibrated dipstick if the position of your fuel tank allows. If you are keen on fitting a fuel gauge, the most reliable tank sensors seem to be the electronic type where the float runs vertically up and down a metal rod installed in the tank through a sealed opening at the top. This is a more robust and seaworthy arrangement than the more mechanical sensor with a float at the end of a pivoting arm.

Electrolysis and sacrificial | 7
anodes

Galvanic corrosion, the insidious eating away of hull fittings caused by the immersion of different metals in an electrolyte such as sea water, is a complex and rather mysterious subject. Different types of boat with different underwater fittings in different sea areas can exhibit marked variation in the degree of electrolysis experienced.

The principle of sacrificial protection is that, since zinc is one of the most active metals in the galvanic series and, with its relatively high voltage potential, is most likely to form an anode and corrode, a zinc sacrificial block will become the focus for galvanic corrosion and waste away safely while your bronze underwater fittings remain untouched.

I must say, touch wood, that we have never found any sign of galvanic action during the 20 years of owning *Stormalong*, most of that time without an anode fitted. Our seacocks are all of good-quality naval bronze, the propeller is bronze, and the original propeller shaft was bronze. The only other metal below the waterline is the iron of the keel, the iron rudder pintles and, recently, the new stainless steel propeller shaft. *Stormalong* is iron fastened, but all the nail heads are well stopped both below and above the waterline, and there had never been any hint of exposure that might cause electrolyte corrosion to any of the bronze nearby.

However, I had been persuaded to install a single sacrificial anode several years ago, just in case. It couldn't do any harm, I thought, and everyone else seemed to have one. Therefore I was intrigued to come across an interesting comment recently in Nigel Calder's excellent book, *Boatowner's Mechanical and Electrical Manual*. He writes: '. . . our boat has been in tropical seawater for five years, completely unbonded and without a single sacrificial zinc anode. The only trace of corrosion is between the bronze propeller and the stainless steel propeller shaft, where it slides in and out of our variable-pitch propeller unit.' This freedom from corrosion accords with our own experience over the years, yet I have heard other yachtsmen tell alarming stories. I particularly remember one Frenchman whose propeller fell off at a crucial moment because of unsuspected electrolytic action.

Apart from natural galvanic corrosion, boats can also suffer from electrolysis set up by battery-powered electric currents leaking from poor insulation or dodgy connections in damp corners of the hull. Stray-current corrosion can be many times more rapid than natural electrolysis, and much more difficult to diagnose and cure. The main preventative measure here is to be extremely conscientious about the quality of all wiring work on board, and the quality of all your basic electrical equipment – such as the cable itself, plugs and sockets, connectors, switches, fuse and distribution panels, junction boxes, and so on.

◆ ELECTRICAL BONDING

When using a sacrificial zinc block to protect underwater fittings against electrolytic corrosion, you are really trying to provide a preferred route for either galvanic or leaking electric currents, such that the zinc is the most likely metal to form an anode and thus be slowly eaten away. Now if all your vulnerable fittings were connected to the sacrificial zinc by wire inside the boat, this preferred electrical path would presumably be taken in all circumstances and the zinc would always form a safely corroding anode in relation to any other underwater metal. This is why, when sacrificial anodes are fitted, the instructions recommend that you at least make a wired connection between the anode and your sterntube, and (see Fig 7.1) between the anode and the propeller shaft.

In fact, there are various schools of thought about the wisdom of bonding fittings together. A possible danger from bonding arises if zinc anodes are not renewed in good time. You then have a situation in which your different metal fittings, immersed in an electrolyte, have been deliberately linked by a good conductor – the ideal circumstances for galvanic current to flow and for corrosion to start taking place in the least noble metal, which effectively becomes the anode for a homemade battery.

On the other hand, if underwater fittings are not wired together but instead are electrically isolated (as far as possible) from each other and from other metal on board, the scope for electrolytic action between them is much reduced. Although different fittings acquire different voltage potentials simply from immersion in sea water, these potentials tend to remain stable in the immediate vicinity of each fitting rather than trying to equalise through the water, which is actually quite a poor electrical conductor.

When trying to prevent galvanic corrosion, you are caught to some extent between taking definite electrical action and making a thorough job

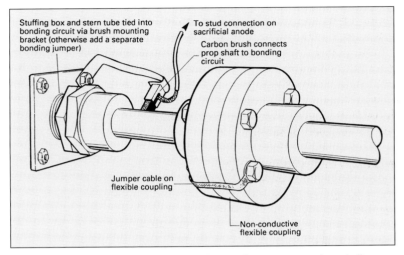

Fig 7.1 Making sure that propeller shaft and sterntube are connected to a hull mounted anode.

of it, or doing nothing, which can be better than doing something badly. In practice, much seems to depend on the quality of metal in your under-water fittings, how close they are together, whether the boat is moored in real salty sea water or a mixture of salt and fresh, and how fast the water usually flows.

MG Duff International Ltd are the sacrificial anode specialists in the UK and the best people to talk to if you are uncertain about whether you need protection and, if so, how many anodes might be required, where to mount them, and how to wire them up. In one of their information sheets, MG Duff confirm the rather capricious nature of electrolytic corrosion:

> The results of corrosion are well known but often unpredictable. On one vessel a rudder stock will wear through in a season; on another a similar part will last 20 years. Propellers may give many years service (though in fact slow breakdown is always going on), but equally they may become corroded and unserviceable within a few months.

MG Duff seem to regard the highest-risk fittings as propellers and propeller shafts, metal rudders and rudder hangings, and mild steel bilge-keels. Skin-fittings are certainly susceptible to electrolytic action, but, if they are of good-quality bronze and isolated from other metals, it is perhaps sufficient to inspect them from time to time, especially the through-hull bolts, and to leave well alone if there are no obvious signs of corrosion.

For the purpose of assessing the likely requirements for anode protection, M G Duff define four classes of boat, depending on their propeller and rudder configurations. *Stormalong* seems to fall into M G Duff Type A, which includes: '. . . single-screw boats with a very short length of propeller shaft exposed to the water and fitted with GRP or wooden rudders.'

As a general rule for this class of boat, one anode will probably be needed for propeller and propeller shaft protection, although older boats with mild-steel rudder hangings like *Stormalong* may also need separate anodes on each side of the rudder to protect these fittings from corrosion. The main anode for protecting the propeller and shaft should be located on the hull bottom below the turn of the bilge, its fore-and-aft position roughly equidistant between the engine gearbox and the inboard end of the stern tube. It should be wired inside the hull as shown in Fig 7.2. Bilge keels can be protected by fitting anodes directly to the steel on each side of both keels.

M G Duff Type B boats are '. . . twin-screwed with long lengths of propeller shaft exposed to the water and supported by shaft brackets.'

Here you will need to fit two anodes under the hull, one to protect each shaft assembly. Bronze or stainless steel rudders, or GRP rudders with bronze or stainless steel stocks, will need to be bonded to the same anode,

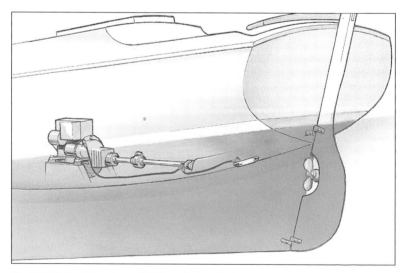

Fig 7.2 MG Duff Type A sacrificial anode installation.

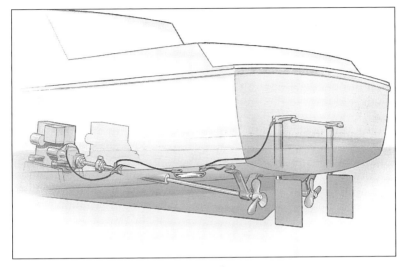

Fig 7.3 MG Duff Type B sacrificial anode installation.

as shown in Fig 7.3. Mild steel rudders will require their own anodes, one fitted either side of each rudder.

M G Duff Type C boats are '. . . single-screwed with a long length of propeller shaft exposed to the water and supported by a shaft bracket, having GRP rudder(s) with bronze or stainless steel stocks.'

As a rule, you can simply fit one anode to protect the propeller, shaft and rudder(s), as shown in Fig 7.4. Encapsulated or cast iron keels need no additional protection, although mild steel bilge-keels should be fitted with their own anodes, one either side of each keel.

M G Duff Type D boats '. . . are those fitted with Sail Drive legs or Stern Drives.' Many of these propulsion units will already be fitted with sacrificial anodes specially designed for their particular shape and combination of metals (see Fig 7.5). However, where no anodes appear to be fitted or seem too small to be effective over long periods, M G Duff usually recommend that a separate anode is fitted to the hull and bonded to the transom plate. With Sail Drive or Stern Drives though, it's important to discuss any proposed anode protection in detail with both the drive manufacturer and with a specialist such as M G Duff. Complex electrolytic reactions can occur between different alloys and you need to be sure of the possible effects of any suggested anode protection before going ahead. Getting it wrong could be costly and potentially dangerous.

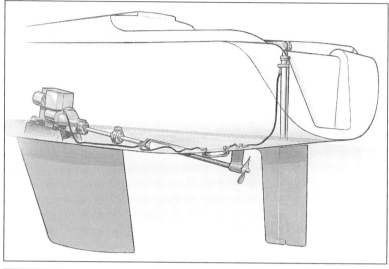

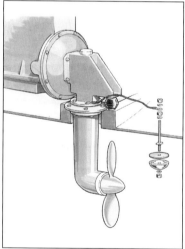

Figs 7.4 & 7.5 MG Duff sacrificial anode installation for Type C boats (above) and Type D boats (left).

With either a Sail Drive unit or a Stern Drive, you particularly have to make sure that the propeller itself has adequate anode protection. Many of the more sophisticated modern props are made of unusual metals or quite complex alloys, and while some are now fitted with their own anodes, they are often quite small and may not even last a full season in some conditions.

◆ PROPELLER SHAFT ANODES

A small rotating zinc anode clamped directly on to the propeller shaft (see Fig 7.4) is the easiest and most reliable way of protecting the shaft from galvanic corrosion. Because the electrical connection is made directly, there is then no need for the rather complicated brush contact or a flexible coupling jumper cable such as that shown in Fig 7.1.

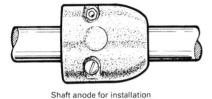

Shaft anode for installation
directly to the propeller shaft

Fig 7.4 A clamp-on shaft anode is the simplest and most reliable way of protecting a prop shaft and propeller.

◆ COOLING JACKET ANODES

Some engines, especially those with raw-water cooling, have a replaceable zinc anode insert for the cooling circuit. If there is any risk of electrolysis between the metal components of an engine, it can certainly be accentuated by hot, fast-flowing sea water. If engine anodes are fitted, they should be checked every season and renewed in good time.

Nigel Calder's excellent book *Boatowner's Mechanical and Electrical Manual* (Adlard Coles Nautical) is informative on most aspects of engine installation and has useful sections on engine controls and galvanic corrosion.

8 | Sea trials

Having worked long and hard on a new engine installation, it can be a nerve-racking occasion when you are finally ready to turn the starter key for the first time. But are you really quite ready? There are some important checks to make before you try to bring the gleaming machinery to life.

◆ FUEL

After filling the diesel tank and switching on the fuel tap, you will need to ensure that the fuel system is completely full of diesel between the tank and the injection pump. Most engines have a hand-priming lever on the fuel lift pump, which allows you to fill the system prior to final bleeding. On our Perkins Perama, there is a bleed plug on the top of the engine-mounted cartridge filter. By unscrewing this plug, you can look into the body of the filter and see when it is full of fuel.

With the main diesel switched on, you operate the hand-priming lever steadily until fuel is drawn along the main supply pipe to fill the water separator, and then further along to fill the cartridge filter. This takes a surprisingly long time using the priming lever, but you should eventually see the fuel level rising in the cartridge filter. When this filter is full and you replace the screw plug, you at least know that the system is full of diesel up to that point.

The Perkins Perama has a bleed nipple down at the injection pump. With this nipple just open half a turn with a spanner, you should continue pumping the priming lever until fuel appears at the nipple, and then tighten up again. You should now have fuel all the way through to the injection pump, after which the engine ought to bleed itself as required. However, if, when you come to start up, the engine runs for a while and then stops, you may have to slacken the bleed nipple, operate the priming pump to expel any air, tighten up, and try the engine again. Sometimes, even after changing the cartridge filter and filling up the system again, I have to repeat this bleeding operation several times before the engine runs and catches.

◆ ENGINE OILS

Before starting up our new engine for the first time, I had considerable discussions with Perkins, with various marine engineers and with several oil manufacturers while I was trying to decide on the right oil with which to fill the new sump of our Perkins Perama. As discussed in Chapter 1, when trying to decide on the right size of engine for your boat, it's important that a diesel should have to work hard most of the time, to avoid the risk of polishing or 'glazing' the cylinder walls through insufficient 'scraping' by the piston rings.

Cylinder glazing can occur with prolonged under-loading of the engine, when the piston rings press too lightly against the cylinder walls and simply polish the deposits from unburnt constituents of the diesel fuel to a shine on the cylinders, rather than grinding a good gas-tight surface. During the early part of a diesel engine's life, you used to be able to increase the risk of cylinder glazing by using an oil with too high a performance – an oil, in other words, which provided too much lubrication. For that reason, when we were filling our sump for the first time, I decided to use a 'cheap and cheerful' marine grade oil with a moderate viscosity. We opted for a heavy-duty HD30 oil for naturally aspirated diesels, supplied by Comma, which was recommended by our local engineer. He said this would 'bed our bores in nicely' and I took his advice seriously, since in his time he had seen the insides of a good many engines affected by glazing.

However, times and technology have changed and there is no longer any need to use 'running-in' oils. These are now really a thing of the past and most oil companies no longer produce such products. The oil grade selected for continued use is now deemed capable of bedding the liners without the need for a running-in oil.

In terms of current oil specifications, the highest-performance, super lubricating oils are now classed as API/CF/SJ, good examples being Castrol Tection T 15W40 or Shell Rimula X Extra 15W-40. Castrol's more run of the mill marine grade oils are those in their MLC range, which are rated to API/CD/SF specification. Castrol MLC 30 is a good general oil for use in most medium- and high-speed marine engines.

For good technical information on marine oils, you can contact the Castrol UK Technical Dept on 01793 512712.

◆ GEARBOX OIL

Some gearboxes use the same kind of oil as the engine, but our Hurth HBW50 box needs Automatic Transmission Fluid (ATF) Type A. This is a very light oil, slightly pink in colour, and the capacity of the box is only 0.3 litres. You need to fill the gearbox with ATF very slowly, checking the dipstick regularly, since only the very bottom part of the dipstick is immersed in oil when it is at the correct level. It is therefore easy to over-fill the gearbox, since the level appears on the dipstick quite suddenly.

◆ ENGINE COOLANT

Most fresh-water cooled engines use a mixture of 'anti-freeze' type coolant and water, normally mixed 50/50. When you first fill the heat exchanger with coolant, you should make up this 50/50 cocktail in a clean container and make sure the coolant and water are thoroughly mixed before pouring into the header tank. Don't overfill with the coolant, since the excess will simply squirt out through the overflow pipe when the engine reaches oper-ating temperature. Follow the manufacturer's directions precisely.

◆ STERNTUBE GREASER

This will not apply to that many engines – where the propeller shaft and its bearings are water lubricated – but we had retained our original sterngear, with its packing-box gland and large grease reservoir mounted up in the cockpit. By turning down the greaser every so often, grease is forced down a flexible pipe into the packing box and back down the pro-peller shaft to the outer bearing cutless. Before running the engine, we have to make sure that the reservoir is full and the greaser ready to use.

◆ STARTING UP

The big moment has now arrived. Check that the fuel is on, the cooling water is on, and batteries are switched to 'both'. Ensure the Morse single-lever control is in neutral, pull out the throttle-only button, and select about a quarter throttle. Now put the starting key in, switch on, and turn to the 'glow plug' position for 20–30 seconds. This operates the heater plugs in each cylinder for cold starting. I turned the switch to 'start' and our new Perkins Perama burst instantly into life. There was a slight hesita-tion as a couple of small air bubbles in the fuel system cleared themselves, and then we were running smoothly. It was a strange sensation, after the gleaming engine had been sitting silently on board for so long. I made sure that the oil pressure and charging lights had gone out and then peered over the stern to check the cooling water. A good flow was being ejected in hefty bursts and the exhaust had a healthy burble. The water temperature gauge hadn't yet moved up from cold, but it would take a little while before the fresh-water circuit reached operating temperature, especially while we were running in neutral. I had left the engine box off in the saloon and my father was looking over the engine to make sure that everything was working as it should. Before starting up, we had checked the alternator belt (which also drives the fresh water pump) for tightness. Now we examined all fuel pipes carefully for weeps around the various unions. I spotted one slight weep at the outlet side of the water separator and pinched the nut up a bit tighter. Otherwise, everything seemed OK.

Then I throttled right back and pushed in the 'throttle only' button prior to checking the gearshift. We were moored securely fore-and-aft, so I moved the control lever ahead and we slipped smoothly into gear. As we took up the strain on the aft warps, I opened the throttle and the propeller stream pushed out powerfully from under the stern. Once you are motoring ahead at a steady speed at which there is minimal movement of the engine on its flexible mounts, the first problem to check for is vibration in the transmission. First, taking great care that no loose clothing can catch anywhere, you should lay a hand on the gearbox to make sure that the propeller shaft is turning smoothly. Then I felt the Aquadrive and its thrust bearing, and finally the sterngland where the propeller shaft disappears through the stern.

Everything was smooth and you could feel no movement whatsoever at the sterngland. This showed the Aquadrive was doing its job of isolating the sterngear and hull from all engine vibration. All we were left with was the shaft turning smoothly in its tube. I gradually opened the throttle to 1800 revs and checked for vibration again. All seemed well. Then I throttled right back, shifted into neutral, and then astern, repeating the procedure to check for vibration. Everything seemed satisfactory, and by the time I had finished these checks the engine had more or less reached operating temperature; I could then check the idling speed.

The idling revs were a shade fast, so I set them down to 1000 revs *using the throttle stop*. Do not, under any circumstances, try to make any speed adjustments other than the straightforward matter of where the throttle arm comes up against its stop. This is achieved simply by slackening a lock nut, turning the throttle stop set screw with a spanner until you settle at the right idling revs, and then tightening up the lock nut again.

◆ UNDER WAY

Before reaching this stage of casting off for the first time, I had had discussions with many people on how best to 'run the engine in'. Some engineers said that diesels didn't really need running in – one old hand at Perkins pointed out that the company made engines for JCB diggers, and that the drivers on building sites weren't usually too worried about how their diggers were run in. However, as expensive items of commercial plant, JCBs are usually coated for a relatively short working life, while owners of new yacht engines will be more concerned with looking after their engines over the longer term.

The consensus of opinion seems to be that the best running in for a new diesel such as ours would be if you had to motor across the Channel during a calm passage, and then had to motor back again. For the first five hours, you'd want to keep the engine working steadily hard, but not overdoing it, at around 60 per cent of maximum rated revs, but varying the throttle setting every so often within a couple of hundred revs above and below. The maximum revs of the Perkins Perama are 3600, so I was running at between 2000 and 2200 revs for this initial period.

After this five hours of 'loosening up', it would be wise to increase the revs to around 70 per cent of maximum, say to 2500 for the Perama, in order to keep the engine working and avoid any risk of polishing the bores. I used this cruising speed for the next 20 hours, since this seemed to be working the engine well enough to prevent glaze but not overstressing until things had loosened up a bit further. After running the engine for 25 hours, I was happy to take the engine up to 80 per cent of maximum every so often, ie to 2800–2900 revs.

◆ MAXIMUM REVS

After this 25 hour run-in, I was also happy to see whether we could reach our rated maximum of 3600 revs. The engine is designed to be able to run continuously at this speed, and an important test of whether you have chosen the right propeller is just being able to reach maximum revs, within about a hundred revs. If you cannot get anywhere near maximum, your propeller is probably too coarsely pitched, and if you can easily reach 3600 and the engine would spin a bit faster if you let her, the propeller is too finely pitched. In fact, with the throttle hard open, the rev counter went up to 3550 revs, which confirmed my earlier view that the propeller was about right.

Since then, my policy has been to keep the engine working hard whenever it is being run at all. As a general rule, I try not to leave the engine idling either in neutral or at slow cruising speeds for any longer than necessary. If possible, when running the engine just to charge the batteries, I like to run in gear as close to normal cruising speed as possible, although this would obviously depend on where you are moored and whether this would cause inconvenience to anyone else.

◆ CONTINUAL CHECKS

As well as carrying out the normal daily checks on oil levels, freshwater level and the alternator belt tightness, and then keeping an eye on the instruments and turning down the sterngland greaser while the engine is running, I think it is a good idea to watch the engine in action every so often. Periodically, and especially when the engine is running for long periods, I often peer into the engine compartment simply to check that:

- There is no sign of any transmission vibration, either at the gearbox, the Aquadrive or the propeller shaft.
- There is no sign of diesel weeps at any of the fuel pipe unions.
- There are no oil or water leaks anywhere.

If there is any small problem such as a slightly weeping fuel union, better to catch it while it *remains* a small problem. And I never forget what a seasoned marine engineer used to tell me whenever I went along looking for some unlikely spare part from our old petrol engine: 'Engines aren't just machines, you know. They like to be *looked* at now and again, and a friendly pat with an oily rag never did any harm.'

9 | Using a power take-off (PTO)

Most modern marine diesels have the facility for adding one or more power take-off (PTO) pulleys at the front of the engine, which can then be used to drive auxiliary equipment such as a second alternator, a hydraulic pump for an anchor winch, a compressor pump for a fridge, a sea water pump for a deck wash hose or emergency bilge pump, and so on.

The idea of tapping some 'free power' from your engine can be appealing. As your engine is running anyway, what better than having it take the strain out of hauling the anchor, or working away steadily at chilling your wines or beers ready for lunch. But in engineering, as in everything else, you rarely get something for nothing. Before you decided on the size and type of your new engine, you had to calculate how much power it needed to provide in order to drive your boat up to her hull speed – allowing for a suitable reserve of power for adverse weather and emergencies.

While it was important not to underpower your boat, it was equally important not to overpower, since a marine diesel is better off working hard throughout its life. As we saw in Chapter 1, an engine should be chosen such that it would normally be working at between 75–85 per cent of maximum horsepower. Keeping some power in reserve, this means that perhaps only 10–15 per cent of maximum power is available for driving auxiliary equipment.

The engineering of a PTO pulley needs to be taken just as seriously as that of the engine installation itself, since the design and alignment of a PTO can have important implications for the long-term wear and performance of the engine. Accurate alignment of PTO pulleys with the engine drive pulley is perhaps the easiest requirement to appreciate, but equally important is the degree of side tension being exerted on the engine drive pulley and, hence, on the crankshaft and its bearings. Fig 9.1 shows how this tension is applied and how the bending moment on the crankshaft is affected by the degree of overhang of the engine drive pulley.

There is obviously a limit to how much side load can be applied to the crankshaft without causing excessive wear on bearings and eventual distortion of the shaft. Most engine manufacturers should be able to supply

An engine with a second alternator driven from a PTO pulley. *Photo courtesy of Volvo Penta.*

graphs that show maximum allowable side loads plotted against overhang distance from the cylinder block. Fig 9.2 reproduces the graph that applies to our own Perkins Perama M30, where the load, R, is measured in Newtons of force and the overhang is measured in millimetres. Sometimes it can be feasible to run two auxiliaries using a double drive pulley on the

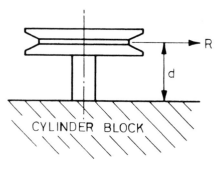

Fig 9.1 Bending moment on the crankshaft.

Bending moment/side loading

The bending moment is the product of the resultant load 'R' acting at a distance of 'd'.

Bending moment: B M = R x d

The face of the cylinder block is used as the datum point for bending moments, both front and rear.

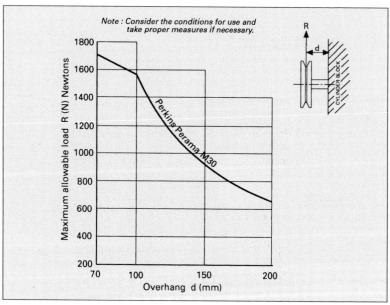

Fig 9.2 Loading at front of crank. *Courtesy of Perkins Group Ltd.*

PTO shaft, providing that the pull of each belt counteracts the other, as shown in Fig 9.3. In this case, the net side load on the crankshaft is much reduced.

In practice, it will not be feasible for most DIY engineers to get involved with accurately measuring the side thrust, in Newtons or anything else, generated by different types and sizes of auxiliary pumps. Instead, it will be more practical to 'clear' with the engine manufacturer or agent any equipment that you propose using on a PTO, making sure you

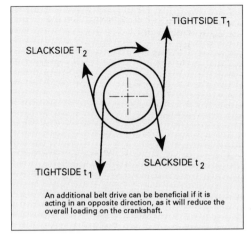

TIGHTSIDE T_1

SLACKSIDE T_2

SLACKSIDE t_2

TIGHTSIDE t_1

An additional belt drive can be beneficial if it is acting in an opposite direction, as it will reduce the overall loading on the crankshaft.

Fig 9.3 Opposing drive belt tensions. *Courtesy of Perkins Group Ltd.*

talk to a sound technician who knows his stuff. One important consideration is that you should only install auxiliary belt-driven equipment that will not invalidate your engine's warranty, and this is obviously best confirmed in writing with the manufacturer.

The critical dimensions for calculating crankshaft side loading are as follows:

- Engine rpm
- Driver pulley diameter (in mm)
- Driven pulley diameter (in mm)
- PTO power requirement of the driven equipment (expressed in kW)
- The PTO direction (degrees clockwise from top dead centre)
- Distance between driver pulley and face of cylinder block (mm)
- Type of pulley (eg 36 degree Vee)
- Type and number of belts.

The measurements and intended mounting arrangements can be set out in a simple diagram, from which your engine manufacturer will be able to assess whether the application you are considering can safely be driven from the PTO pulley. For those interested in following the mathematics, an example of a crankshaft side loading calculation is given in Appendix 1.

◆ ENGINE MANUFACTURERS' PTO KITS

Most engine manufacturers can supply a bolt-on assembly kit for mounting compact PTO auxiliaries such as second alternators, deck wash pumps, hydraulic pumps or fridge compressors, or sometimes such kits are available from the supplier of the auxiliary equipment. It is always advisable to use such kits if possible, since the engineering should have been carefully thought out to make the installation both relatively straightforward and, most important, safe to use.

On this last point, always bear in mind that the front end of an engine, with its high-revving pulleys and spinning drive belts, is potentially a very dangerous place. Many nasty accidents happen each year in which loose clothing, long hair, ties, watchstraps, and even medallions on chains, become caught in belts or pulleys. You can imagine some of the dreadful consequences, so always take extraordinary care when examining an engine while it is running, and never attempt to make adjustments with the engine running.

As far as the basic engineering is concerned, any auxiliary equipment to be belt-driven from a PTO has to be securely bolted to the engine block

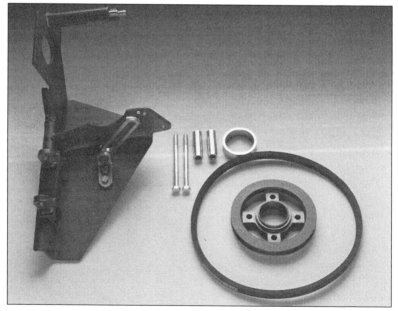

A Volvo Penta kit for adding belt-driven auxiliary equipment.

so that the drive and driven pulleys are exactly aligned. The engineering needs to be sound with no hint of the Heath Robinson about it.

◆ BELT TENSION

The mounting system has to provide the correct belt tension, which can be considerable at high engine revs when the auxiliary equipment is fully loaded. Drive belt tension is always a compromise between too much, which can damage the shaft bearings in pumps or alternators by excessive side loading; or too little, allowing belt slippage at high powers and speeds, causing excessive belt and pulley wear. You need to be able to adjust the tension easily, since belts naturally stretch in the normal course of service. There are two practical methods of adjustment:

- By having the mounting position of the driven equipment adjustable on a sliding arm, just like the system generally used with engine-driven alternators.
- By using an 'idler pulley', which is a lazy pulley whose sole purpose is to pull the belt outwards and take up slack. Idler pulleys can either be adjustable manually or be springloaded to supply the right tension automatically.

The usual method of setting belt tension, shown in most engine manuals, is by pressing sideways at the middle of the longest run of belt between two of the pulleys and then adjusting the tension such that the belt will deflect by a given distance (see Fig 9.4). For example, to adjust the alternator belt for our Perkins Perama, the manual says that the tension is just right when

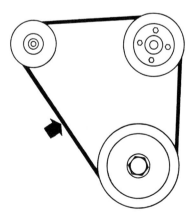

Fig 9.4 Assessing belt tension. The usual method of estimating belt tension is by applying pressure in the centre of the longest run of belt between any two pulleys, and adjusting the tension until the belt deflects by a given amount.

The correct deflection for your engine should be given in the manufacturer's handbook or workshop manual.

a force of 1 kg (just over 2 lb) deflects the centre of the longest run of belt by 5 mm (just under ¼ in).

This instruction sounds more precise than can usually be achieved in practice, since one does not always have the wherewithal to produce a convenient force of exactly 1 kg. You can try to imagine the equivalent weight of a bag of sugar, but this can be a bit tricky when pushing sideways with one hand and, at the same time, holding a ruler across the belt with your other hand to try to gauge the deflection.

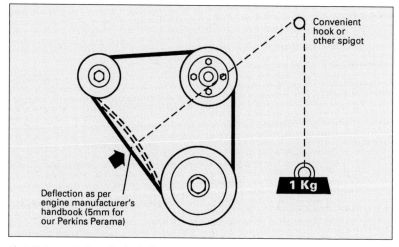

Convenient hook or other spigot

1 Kg

Deflection as per engine manufacturer's handbook (5mm for our Perkins Perama)

Fig 9.5 A practical method of adjusting belt tension.

Some mechanics use a small spring balance for these adjustments, pulling the belt across with the balance hook until the scale reads 1 kg while measuring the deflection with a steel tape. However, one practical method is to tie a piece of string to the middle of the belt, as in Fig 9.5. Now lead the string over some convenient makeshift 'pulley' – a cup-hook in the galley perhaps, or anything suitably smooth – and hang a kilogram weight from the end of the string. You can then measure the belt deflection, with both hands free, when this weight comes on to the string.

Most engineers will adjust a drive belt by experience, tightening up until it feels 'just right', nicely taut but not bar taut. Although it is often convenient to use a lever, such as a long screwdriver, to hold the alternator or pump across in the right position until you can tighten the holding bolts, you must always use such levers with control and circumspection.

◆ ENGINE-DRIVEN FRIDGE COMPRESSORS

I always think that producing 'cold' is a mysterious business and we rather take for granted our fridges at home – they are just there, they are switched on all the time, and they work. We don't concern ourselves with how much power they consume or how they operate. Many boats now have small 12V or 24V fridges that are regarded in much the same way, except that any power consumption aboard a boat is always a nagging worry.

So there is much to be said for a fridge or cold box compartment that is automatically chilled whenever the engine is running. With good insulation, this facility can be extremely handy when cruising, even for sailing boats that only use their engines relatively infrequently. How does such a fridge work, though, and what sort of equipment is needed to drive it?

In order to keep a fridge compartment cold, what you are doing is continuously removing heat. The mechanism is designed to absorb heat from within the compartment, take it away, and then dissipate the heat outside the compartment. The basic principle of refrigeration is demonstrated if you spill some highly volatile liquid, such as methylated spirit, over your hand. After a few seconds, your hand starts to feel cold as the meths evaporates and draws the necessary energy as heat from your skin.

If you were to keep on trickling meths on to your hand, you would continue, as it were, to be refrigerated. Were it possible to devise a closed system in which the evaporated vapour of the coolant could be distilled back into liquid and reused, you would have the essential elements of a refrigerator.

However, the evaporation even of spirits such as meths is a pretty slow business. What is needed to speed up the process is a liquid that boils at what we would normally regard as 'freezing' temperatures. A suitable coolant used in fridges nowadays is Tetrafluorethane (R134A), whose boiling point at average atmospheric pressure is around $-27°$ C. Pressure is a critical factor in the process, since the temperature at which a liquid boils is directly related to pressure. The higher the pressure acting upon a liquid, the less easily it vaporises and the higher the boiling point.

A basic refrigerator uses a compressor and condenser to force the coolant into its liquid form, which then flows through a series of pipes, known as the evaporator, within the fridge compartment. The evaporator absorbs heat, thereby cooling the compartment down, and vaporised coolant returns through the system to the compressor which, in conjunction with the condenser, converts the coolant back to a liquid.

Using this system, the compressor runs until the evaporator has been cooled to the level set by the thermostat, at which point the compressor switches off. The cold evaporator works upon the contents of the fridge to cool them down and keep them cool but, in so doing, warms itself up. The thermostat therefore switches the compressor on again and the cooling cycle continues.

While this constant-cycling system is suitable for a domestic fridge, where power for the compressor is continually available, the circumstances aboard a boat are rather more demanding. If the compressor is to be driven directly by the engine, rather than by using precious battery power, it is desirable to have some means of storing 'cold' while the engine is running, which is then used to keep the fridge compartment cool when the engine is off.

This storage can be achieved by using a 'eutectic plate', often known simply as a cold plate or holding plate. With this system, the evaporator is immersed in a sealed container which contains a second coolant that alternates between solid and liquid form, rather than between liquid and vapour. Just as conversion from liquid into vapour requires the input of heat, so does the conversion from solid into liquid – for example, the conversion of ice into water. In this case, the heat required for conversion is known by physicists as the 'latent heat of fusion'.

A eutectic plate contains an outer liquid coolant which solidifies at a very low temperature. A compressor and condenser are used as before, for refrigerating the inner coolant that is pumped through a 'cold exchanger' immersed in the outer coolant. For marine applications, the compressor can be belt-driven by the engine, and the condenser is usually cooled by raw water diverted from the engine cooling system. The evaporator freezes the liquid in the plate into solid form, extracting the latent heat of fusion as the liquid solidifies, so that you end up with a cold block of solid within the eutectic plate. This provides an effective storage of coldness within the fridge compartment.

The eutectic plate gradually absorbs heat from the compartment, thereby cooling it down. The solid within the plate melts slowly, absorbing latent heat of fusion until all the coolant has been converted into liquid

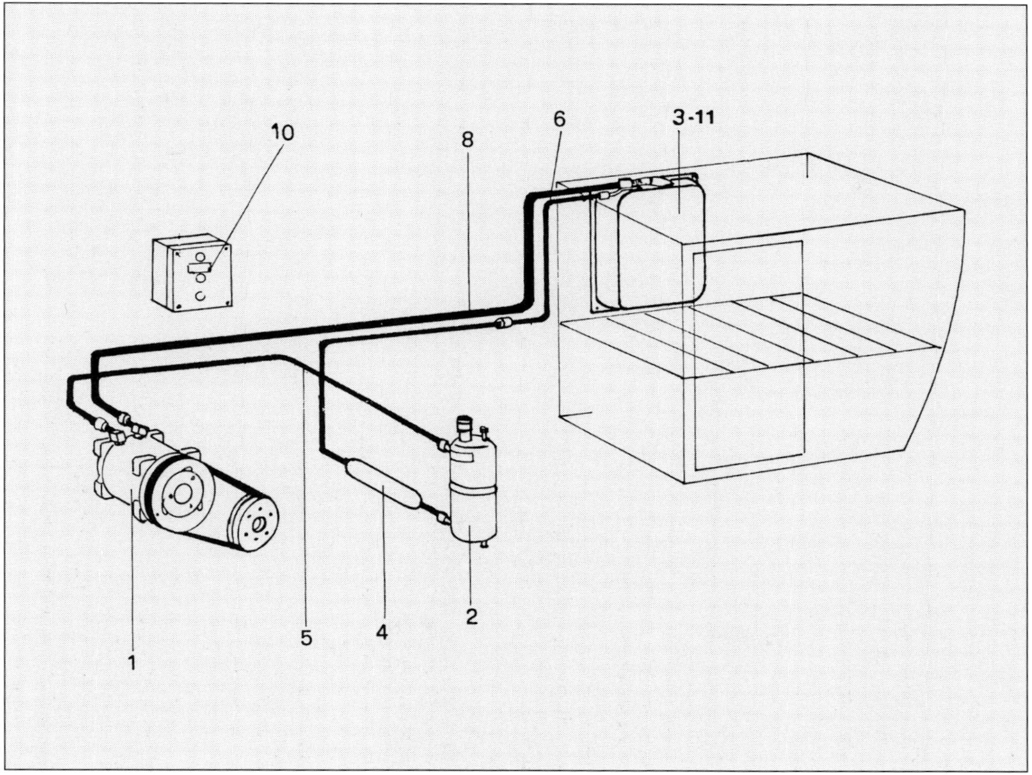

Fig 10.1 The basic components of an engine-driven holding-plate fridge circuit. *Courtesy of Penguin Engineering Ltd.*

Key

1 Engine-driven compressor
2 Condenser with pressure switch
3 Holding plate, installed in fridge compartment
4 Dryer
5 Hose C discharge
6 Pipe B liquid
8 Hose A suction
10 Electronic thermostat

and the temperature of the plate starts to rise. This melting process is normally slow enough to take you through to the next occasion on which the engine is run.

Perhaps the best known marine holding plate refrigerators are the 'Frigoboat' systems, which are distributed in the UK by Penguin Refrigeration Ltd of Southampton. An important advantage of these systems is that, with the right insulation, any convenient locker or space within the boat can be converted into an effective fridge by installing a holding plate of adequate capacity.

A circuit diagram for a single-plate installation is shown in Fig 10.1. The condenser is cooled by diverting part of the engine's raw cooling water, so that no extra skin-fittings are needed in the hull. Its purpose is to help condense the outer coolant from vapour form back into liquid, ready for recirculation within the system, and to dissipate heat from the fridge circuit into the cooling water circuit. Fig 10.2 shows a Frigoboat compressor mounting kit for a Volvo 28 hp diesel. Such kits are available for many different makes and models of engine.

This kind of refrigeration can be highly effective for sailing boats, so long as the fridge compartment is well insulated and you use a large enough holding plate for the capacity of the compartment. With a well-installed system, it should be possible to 'charge' the holding plate with cold with an hour or so of engine running, and the plate should then stay cold for the next 24 hours.

◆ FRIDGE INSTALLATION TIPS

ELECTRICS

Basic electrics are often a weakness and probably account for 75 per cent of marine fridge failures. Main supply cables from the batteries to the DC distribution panel are frequently undersized; perhaps they seemed large enough when first installed, but more and more auxiliary equipment tends to be added aboard boats, and you can reach a point where supply cables cannot take the required current.

It is not much good spending a considerable sum on a new fridge system and then failing to provide the necessary electrical power. Sound electrics are equally important for belt-driven fridges, which need a reliable supply for their control systems and for the electromagnetic clutch that cuts the compressor in and out.

FITTING THE CONDENSER

Fridge condensers are normally quite compact and easy to install, and most obtain their cooling water via a bypass valve fitted in the raw-water circuit just on the outlet side of the impeller pump. The valve acts as a venturi and

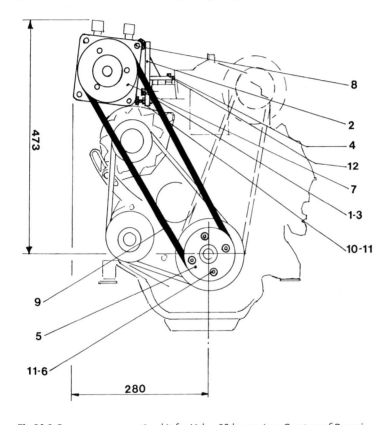

Fig 10.2 Compressor mounting kit for Volvo 28 hp engine. *Courtesy of Penguin Engineering Ltd.*

Key

1 Original screw M8 (2)
2 Compressor bracket (1)
3 TC M8 x 25 allen screw (2)
4 TC M8 x 70 allen screw (2)
5 Pulley A293002 (1)

6 TC M8 x 40 allen screw (4)
7 Frigoboat compressor (1)
8 TC M10 x 110 allen screw (1)
9 Belt A47 (1)
10 TC M8 x 50 allen screw (1)
11 TC M8 x 75 allen screw (4)

creates a small pressure difference – enough with our size of engine to pump about a gallon of water per minute to the condenser. The water returns to the same valve and thence continues its journey through the engine heat exchanger and out to the exhaust bend.

For smaller engines, say up to 10 hp, it is usually best to dispense with a bypass valve and send all the raw water through the condenser first, on its way to the engine. For large engines, such as big Gardners, which sometimes have a surplus of raw water being pumped through, you can use a straightforward T-piece after the impeller pump in order to divert a proportion of the inlet flow to the condenser and then discharge over the side via its own outlet.

INSULATING MATERIAL

The insulating material for constructing a fridge box needs to be carefully selected. Polystyrene is not a good choice, so don't be tempted to use the kind of foam in which hi-fi or other electronic equipment is packed. Polyurethane is best, but you must provide a water-vapour barrier outside the fridge container, otherwise the container and/or the surrounding area will quickly become soaked with moisture. This barrier, which can be of metal or GRP, is particularly important for wooden boats, otherwise your fridge can cause nearby timber to become saturated and vulnerable to rot.

When you are choosing the material for a fridge compartment, it is worth getting in touch with your local Scott-Bader depot, whose address and phone number you should easily find in the *Yellow Pages*. Scott-Bader are well versed in the various insulating materials available and should be able to supply the best insulation for your particular application at a reasonable price.

SIDE- OR TOP-LOADING FRIDGE?

Contrary to popular belief, side-loading fridges are generally no less efficient than top-loading ones. It is often said that whenever you open a vertical fridge door, all the cold air rushes out at the bottom and escapes, so the compressor then has to work harder to replace the cold. While it is true that a certain amount of cold air will escape each time you open the door, the amount of 'cold' carried by this air is pretty negligible compared with the cold stored in the much heavier items stored in the fridge. These will retain their low temperature for a considerable time with the door open, and it doesn't take the eutectic plate long to bring down the air temperature again once the door is shut.

With a top-loading fridge, on the other hand, although very little cold air is lost when you open the lid, you are liable to lose much more cold when removing various items from the top of the compartment to get at what you want, which invariably seems to be at the bottom. Also, top-loaders are often located right in the corner of the galley and difficulty of access can mean that the lid is open for much longer than would be the case with a side-loader.

The main advantage of top-loading compartments is the more secure stowage. There is no risk of food falling out at sea when you open the lid, while a side-loader can be a menace if the boat is heeled the wrong way. Fridge doors, well stacked with bottles, can also make lethal weapons as they swing around while you are trying to get something out. Whether you opt for a side- or top-loading fridge, make sure that you have a good seal around the door or lid.

DRAINHOLES

When you convert an ordinary ice box into a fully fledged fridge, you will not need the drainhole that has usually been provided. On the contrary, drainholes can be a source of inefficiency and trouble, allowing into the fridge the ingress of heat, diesel smells from the bilge, and so on, and letting bits of food down into the bilge to rot. Better to block the drain-hole permanently and simply use a sponge when you want to mop out the compartment.

PLUMBING

Most holding-plate systems are supplied complete with the necessary piping and hose runs. Frigoboat units, for example, including piping, are all factory charged with refrigerant, while the pipe lengths have self-sealing couplings for easy connection for all components without any refrigerant loss. Fridge plumbing should be neatly clipped along a safe but accessible route where there is little risk of accidental damage, and preferably as clear as possible of heat sources such as engine, cooker or stove.

USEFUL ADDRESSES

- Penguin Marine Refrigeration Ltd, Unit 6, Second Avenue Business Park, Millbrook, Southampton SO15 0LP. Tel (02380) 779800.
- Scott-Bader Co Ltd, Wollaston, Wellingborough, Northants NN29 7RL. Tel (01933) 663100.

◆ BILGE AND DECK WASH PUMPS

One of the simplest belt-driven auxiliaries that can be fitted to a marine engine is a sea-water flexible impeller pump, either for bilge pumping or for supplying a deck wash hose. In fact, the same pump can be used for both these purposes (although not at the same time) by using suitable diverter valves on both the inlet and the outlet sides of the pump (see Fig 10.3). Since a modest-sized impeller pump will absorb relatively little power compared with the power of the engine, there will usually be no worries about overloading the crankshaft pulley for this application.

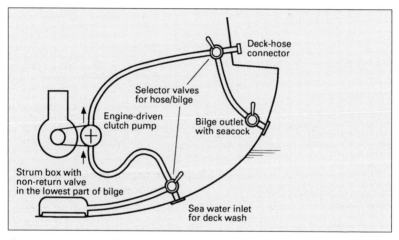

Fig 10.3 Diverter seacock arrangement for providing deck wash and bilge pumping from the same engine-driven pump.

One of the characteristics of flexible impeller pumps is that they must not be allowed to run dry, so for bilge pumping you need to have some arrangement whereby the pump can be stopped as soon as the bilges are empty. The simplest way of achieving this is by using a clutch pump, which is simply declutched to switch the pump off. The belt and pump drive pulley will continue to run, but decoupled from the pump shaft and impeller. The clutches on such pumps can be operated manually or electromagnetically, and either type can be operated remotely from the cockpit or wheelhouse – with the manual type using a push-pull cable rather like an engine stop control.

If a flexible impeller pump is to be used for bilge pumping but is not

One-inch manual clutch pump.
*Courtesy: Cleghorn Waring & Co
(Pumps) Ltd.*

fitted with a clutch, it will therefore be required to operate continuously whenever the engine is running. In this case, the pump must be lubricated from a separate sea-water connection or bleed-off arrangement from the engine's raw-water cooling circuit, to prevent dry running when the bilges are empty. This is rather a complicated and not a particularly satisfactory arrangement, so a clutch-pump, either manual or electromagnetic, is very much preferable.

The Jabsco range of bronze-cased impeller pumps is perhaps the most well known, built to a heavy-duty specification for marine use. The photograph above shows a Jabsco pump with a manual clutch, suitable for service as a deck wash or emergency bilge pump. Various pump capacities are available, from 80 l (17½ gal) per minute at 1500 rpm for the Jabsco 51080 series with 1 in BSP (2.5 cm) ports, up to 270 l (about 59½ gal) per minute at 1500 rpm for the 51270 series pump with 2 in BSP (5 cm) ports.

If you are going to the trouble of fitting a belt-driven pump, I would recommend installing one of generous rather than miserly capacity. It can be reassuring to know in an emergency such as a collision – which may have left you with a serious leak in the hull – that you have a hefty engine-driven pump available to remove large quantities of water so long as there is diesel in the tank.

For bilge pumping, the water inlet will be a ribbed flexible pipe leading from the lowest part of the bilge, where a strum box with a non-return valve should be fitted. Although the Jabsco clutch pumps are self-priming to a head of about 4 m (13 ft), it is best for their long-term life if the impeller starts to draw water immediately they are running. The pump outlet will be a standard skin-fitting, probably at the side of the hull several inches above water level. The outlet skin-fitting should have a seacock or non-return valve, but always make sure that any outlet is open before engaging the pump.

For deck wash pumping, you need a sea water inlet with at least the same bore as the pump ports. This will probably mean making another hole in the hull and fitting a new seacock, because it is not usually feasible to share the engine raw-water inlet unless this happens to be oversize in the first place. It is important not to restrict the cooling water supply to the engine by drawing off a substantial proportion of the inflow for deck washing. Our Perkins Perama, for example, uses a Jabsco raw-water pump with 18 mm (¾ in) internal diameter ports. Therefore the water inlet and seacock are also 18 mm (¾ in) internal diameter to provide an unrestricted flow. But if you wanted to supply an 80 l (17½ gal) per minute deck wash pump, which has 25 mm (1 in) BSP ports, from the same hole in the hull, this hole would have to be enlarged to take at least a 30 mm (1¼ in) internal diameter seacock (38 mm (1½ in) would be preferable). You could then use a Y-branch to divide the inlet from the seacock, as shown in Fig 10.4.

For some boats, it may be practical to supply a modest deck wash pump from an existing sea-toilet inlet, by substituting the original toilet seacock with a three-way seacock of similar capacity, so that this seacock supplies *either* the toilet inlet or the deck wash pump inlet. However, many

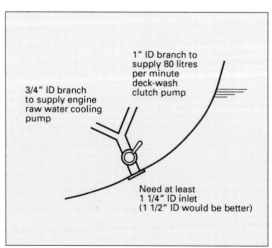

1" ID branch to supply 80 litres per minute deck-wash clutch pump

3/4" ID branch to supply engine raw water cooling pump

Need at least 1 1/4" ID inlet (1 1/2" ID would be better)

Fig 10.4 Shared seawater inlet for engine cooling and deck wash pump. Inlet capacity is proportional to the cross-sectional *area* of the inlet pipe.

toilet inlets are 18 mm (¾ in) bore, which is a bit restricted for a 25 mm (1 in) bore deck wash pump.

Probably the most satisfactory arrangement is for the deck wash pump to be of generous capacity with its own skin-fitting of the correct bore, but you can then use a three-way seacock to switch from deck wash to bilge pumping, as in Fig 10.3. On the outlet side of the pump, you then need an arrangement that can accommodate either a deck hose or a bilge outlet, although there is a risk of making things rather too complicated with diverter valves on the outlet side of the pump as well as the inlet side.

If the bilge pump is intended for emergency use only, perhaps the simplest solution is to install a hose terminal up on deck, with a straightforward screw-on cap for when the pump is not being used. When deck washing, you would connect an ordinary plastic hose to this terminal, as you would in the garden. For bilge pumping, you could keep a shorter length of hose – just long enough to reach over the side – that had its own screw-on connector. However, you would need to ensure that the cap was always removed and the right inlet switched on before the pump was engaged.

◆ HYDRAULIC POWER

Some boatowners are intrigued by the idea of hydraulic power, attracted by the prospect of being able to run a belt-driven hydraulic pump off the engine, and thereby drive such auxiliary equipment as an anchor windlass or perhaps a bow thruster with the advantage of remote fingertip control. While these possibilities are perfectly feasible with quite a modest size of engine, it is important to recognise that hydraulics is an extremely specialist subject with plenty of pitfalls for the uninformed.

It is usually a mistake to imagine that you can pick up a secondhand hydraulic pump at a bargain price from a backstreet garage or perhaps from *Exchange and Mart*, and then bolt this on to the engine to provide an all-purpose source of hydraulic power for driving a bank of auxiliaries. To get the best from hydraulics, you really need to know exactly what you want the installation to achieve, and you also have to be prepared to spend some money to buy the right equipment for the job.

In addition, hydraulic plumbing requires great care and the use of correct pipe, hoses and connectors, since you might be dealing with some very high pressures – perhaps in excess of 2000 lb per square in. If solid pipework is used, it should be cold-drawn seamless tube tested to BS3602

(DIN 2391C). Flexible hose should meet hydraulic standards and the choice of rating will vary according to the maximum system pressure.

Flexible hose to SAE100 R13 will cover almost all applications, although for many hydraulic systems a lower specification may be suitable. Drain-line hoses, suction pipes and oil cooler hoses are subject to far less pressure than the main hydraulics, and can generally use hoses meeting SAE 100 R1 A/AT specification.

Hydraulic runs up to about 12 m (40 ft) would normally use hose of 12 mm (½ in) internal diameter, although this will depend on the power and flow rate of the system. The faster the flow rate, the larger the hose bore required, but 12 mm (½ in) hose should be suitable for flow rates up to about 40 l (nearly 9 gal) per minute. In any event, hydraulic hoses should never be installed with tight bends – not less than 20 cm (8 in) radius for 12 mm (½ in) hose. Hoses should be well clipped right along the run, otherwise the pressure changes can cause them to jump about, with the loss of efficiency and possibly causing chafe.

Cleanliness is an important factor with hydraulics. Even a minute quantity of debris can damage either the hydraulic pump or the motor, which are engineered to very fine tolerances. You should be meticulous, indeed almost surgical, when assembling and connecting hoses, especially when you have to lead long hose runs through lockers or behind bulkheads. Hose terminals should always be capped when they are not connected, to guard against the risk of picking up dirt in the system. New hoses should be flushed through with hydraulic oil before they are finally connected.

HYDRAULIC ANCHOR WINDLASS

Hitherto, the use of hydraulic winches or anchor windlasses has tended to be restricted to larger yachts, where greater and more sustained pulling power is required than can be provided by electric windlasses. Cost is also a constraint, since hydraulic winches and their installations are considerably more expensive than their electric equivalents, which these days are extremely effective and perfectly adequate for normal cruising. However, the owners of longer-distance cruising yachts, even of quite modest size, can benefit from installing a hydraulic anchor windlass, especially where the cruising is to be shorthanded. Modern winch designs are certainly becoming increasingly compact both above and below deck.

The main advantage of hydraulics comes from the ruggedness and inherent long-term reliability of a good-quality installation, and it is for

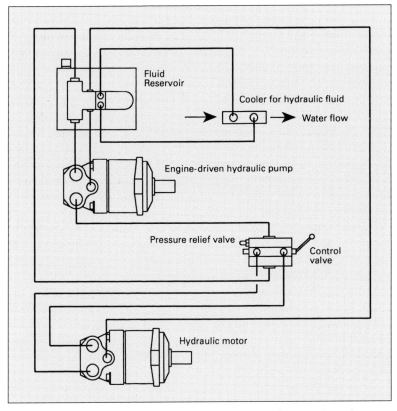

Fig 10.5 Piping diagram for basic hydraulic drive. *Courtesy of ARS Marine Ltd.*

similar reasons that hydraulics are preferred for driving general-purpose winches aboard workboats and fishing boats. But for a yacht in particular, a hydraulic windlass can also provide potentially valuable emergency power, which an electric windlass could not easily match. Such power might be welcome for pulling yourself off a shoal in some far-flung anchorage, or perhaps helping to pull someone else off. With a carefully thought-out arrangement of snatch blocks so that a masthead halyard can be turned on to a warping drum, a hydraulic windlass can also be used to hoist a heavy sail singlehanded, lift a dinghy or outboard up on to the deck, or recover a crew who has fallen overboard.

Fig 10.5 shows a schematic diagram for a typical hydraulic installation. An engine-mounted, belt-driven pump draws hydraulic oil from the reservoir and pumps this fluid under high pressure to the control valve. A leak-off hose returns unused oil – known as 'drain oil' – from the pump to the reservoir at relatively low pressure. An excessive rate of drain oil flow indicates that a pump unit is worn and will soon need reconditioning or replacing.

The control valve acts rather like a three-way tap. In the 'off' position, oil is simply pumped back to the reservoir without doing any work. So while the hydraulic motor is not being used, the pump is continually feeding oil from and back to the reservoir. Therefore for a windlass in the 'haul' position, oil is fed under pressure to the 'haul' inlet port at the hydraulic motor, so that the windlass rotates to pull up the anchor chain. In the 'lower' position, oil is diverted to the reversing port at the motor, so the windlass rotates in the opposite direction to let out chain.

With the most sophisticated (and expensive) types of hydraulic pump, the output pressure can be varied to give variable power and hence variable speed of operation. However, the control valve shown in Fig 10.5 simply reverses the direction of flow of the hydraulic fluid, thereby causing the hydraulic motor to operate in the opposite direction at a fixed power determined by the pump pressure and rate of flow.

Note that the control unit incorporates a pressure-release valve, which operates to release excessive oil pressure in the event of a motor malfunction or if, for example, excessive load were to come on to an anchor windlass while the control valve is open.

HYDRAULIC WINDLASS INSTALLATION

Fig 10.6 illustrates the connections for a vertically mounted chain windlass with a warping capstan, while the photograph shows the smallest hydraulic windlass in the Lewmar range, the elegant and compact 2000 model. To drive this windlass, Lewmar recommend a hydraulic pump capable of producing 120–130 bar of pressure with a flow rate around 21 litres (4.6 gal) per minute. This will achieve the full-load torque of the windlass and give a hauling rate, once the anchor has broken out, of about 16 m (52 ft) per minute, well in excess of the Lloyd's requirement for 9 m (29 ft) per minute.

The capstan drum can be operated separately, either for warping or, via snatch blocks, for hauling halyards, etc. The foot controls would be the same as for an electric windlass – one for 'Up' and one for 'Down'. With the type of hydraulic pumps used for most yacht windlasses, it is not possible to incorporate a variable speed control in the system. However, setting

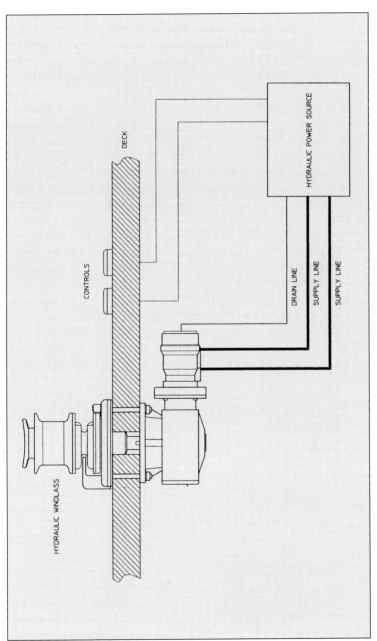

Fig 10.6 Connections for a vertical chain windlass and capstan drum. *Courtesy of Lewmar Marine Ltd.*

the hydraulics to the recommended parameters will give good general-purpose hauling power. With 120 bar pressure and a flow rate of 21 litres (4.6 gal) per minute, this windlass would provide a 900 kg (2000 lb) pull and be taking about 2½ hp from the engine via the belt-driven hydraulic pump.

HYDRAULIC BOW-THRUSTERS

In talking about bow-thrusters, we are now well out of the scope of the smaller engines this book has been concerned with, but it's interesting to look briefly at a hydraulics application which may become smaller-scale and more popular in the future. It is certainly true that, in purely engineering terms and ignoring questions of cost, hydraulics have considerable advantages over electric systems for driving bow-thrusters. As a rule, the electric motors for yacht-rated thrusters can only be used in fairly short bursts of power, otherwise they are prone to burn out. A hydraulic thruster, on the other hand, can be run continuously at full load without risk of damage.

The large motors for the more powerful electric thrusters can be very heavy, whereas equivalent hydraulic motors are much lighter. Also, with electric power, you either have to install a dedicated, and extremely heavy bank of batteries well forward near the thruster unit, or else run very large diameter supply cables from the main batteries in order to avoid significant voltage drop.

One of the most compact, well-engineered and easily installed hydraulic bow-thrusters for yachts between about 36 ft and 50 ft is the

Vetus BOW 95 HM hydraulic bow-thruster.
Courtesy of Vetus den Ouden Ltd.

Hydraulic PTO driven pump for a bow thruster. *Courtesy: Vetus den Ouden Ltd.*

Vetus BOW95HM, which develops 6kW of power at the hydraulic motor. The thruster unit consists of a neat drive-leg, rather like a sail-drive, which is fitted sideways in the bow-thruster tunnel and can run 'forwards' or in 'reverse' to give port or starboard thrust.

The photograph on page 114 shows a BOW95HM thruster unit. Power is drawn from the engine using a hydraulic pump, which on many larger engines can be connected directly by a spline to a convenient power take-off point at the gearbox. Sometimes the pump can be driven from a PTO pulley at the front of the engine.

A note of caution, though. Where, for example, the power consumption of a hydraulic pump without any bow-thruster load is negligible, larger units might well absorb up to 33 kW at maximum load, ie up to about 45 hp. These more powerful systems can therefore only be used with larger engines, typically greater than 100 hp, which can produce this kind of power near idling speed when required.

The Vetus bow-thruster is controlled from the helm position by a port-starboard switch panel or joystick, which operates solenoids to activate the directional control valve at the hydraulic pump. This control valve simply reverses the direction of flow of the hydraulic fluid, which causes the hydraulic motor driving the bow-thruster to change direction.

It's worth remembering that, once you have a workmanlike hydraulic power system installed aboard a larger boat, it's relatively simple to extend the range of applications to, for example, sail-hoisting winches or sheet winches.

11 | Hot-water systems

◆ FITTING A HOT-WATER SYSTEM USING A CALORIFIER

Energy-conscious boatowners are well aware that the hot water discharged over the side through the engine exhaust outlet represents wasted therms that could be put to good use on board. One way of recycling this otherwise wasted heat is to install a hot-water system, using a marine calorifier as a heat exchanger in the engine's fresh-water cooling circuit.

A calorifier is really a heavy-duty, well-insulated water storage tank – rather like a domestic hot-water cylinder, but much more strongly constructed to withstand the internal pressure generated by the pump and the general shocks and vibration of marine use. Inside most calorifiers is a coil of copper pipe, through which the engine's fresh cooling water is pumped. The coil heats up the reservoir of water within the calorifier, which is then pumped off using a pressure pump and a standard marine plumbing system. Vetus calorifiers use a double-walled tank instead of a coil, which gives them a very large heating surface and a short heat-up time.

Once the engine has reached normal running temperature, the fresh water within the engine cooling system circulates at between about 80°C–90°C (176°F–194°F). By adding a calorifier, you are simply extending the length of the fresh-water circuit, which will be driven as before by the engine's fresh-water pump. With water entering the coil at up to 90°C (194°F), you can expect a modern calorifier to provide a full charge of hot water at 60°C (140°F) in less than half an hour.

LOCATION OF THE CALORIFIER

A marine calorifier is quite a bulky item of equipment, with a typical 54.5 litre (12 gal) unit measuring perhaps 762 mm x 457 mm (30 in x 18 in) and needing space around it for securing straps and pipework. Ideally, with standard pumped cooling water circulation, you should install a calorifier with its coil on the same level as, or below, the engine cooling header tank. The calorifier should also be mounted as near the engine as possible, so that the engine's circulation pump has the least possible work to do and you minimise the reduction of flow rate in the system. If you have room in the engine compartment for a calorifier, so much the better, since the pipe runs will be short and the heat from the engine will help to minimise heat loss from the calorifier.

The mounting arrangements for the calorifier need to be strong and well engineered. Remember that a gallon of water weighs 4.5 kg (10 lb), so that a 54½ litre (12 gal) calorifier will weigh about 54.25 kg (120 lb) when full, ie well over a hundredweight. Cleghorn Waring supply two shapes of calorifier: a vertical calorifier, which stands on its own flat base and can be located by fastening down the feet attached to the copper skirt, then securing with stout straps; or a horizontal calorifier, which can be mounted in a cradle and also secured with straps. However, vertical calorifiers must be mounted vertically, and horizontal calorifiers must be mounted horizontally, to avoid air-locking in the coil.

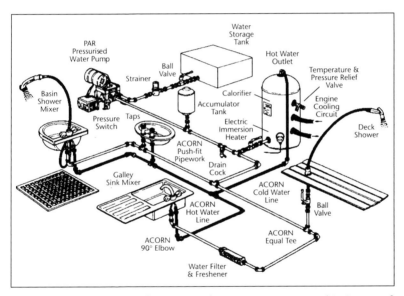

Fig 11.1 Schematic diagram of a pressurised water system (not to scale). *Courtesy of Cleghorn Waring (Pumps) Ltd.*

CALORIFIER CONNECTIONS

Fig 11.1 shows how a marine calorifier fits into a typical pressurised fresh-water system and Fig 11.2 shows an example of the connections to a single-coil vertical calorifier. The cold-water supply arrives at the bottom

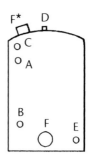

Single Coil Vertical Calorifiers

A = Coil inlet (external thread)
B = Coil outlet (external thread)
C = Temperature & Pressure relief valve (internal thread)
D = Hot water outlet (external thread)
E = Cold water inlet (external thread)/drain
F = Immersion heater boss (2¼ inch BSP internal)

Fig 11.2 Calorifier connection points (schematic). *Courtesy Cleghorn Waring and Co (Pumps) Ltd.*

of the calorifier at connection E, via a ball-valve that can be used to isolate or switch off the hot water part of the circuit. Hot water comes out at the top of the calorifier through connection D and is piped direct to the various hot water taps around the boat. You can see from Fig 11.1 that both the cold- and hot-water systems are driven by the same pressure pump and accumulator tank.

The calorifier has 'in' and 'out' connections (A and B) for the coil, through which water is fed from and back to the engine block. Most modern engines have terminals ready in the block for a hot-water system. To ensure a good water circulation in the engine cooling circuit, pipework of at least 12 mm (½ in) bore should be used, and I would prefer 18 mm (¾ in) bore for our 29 hp Perkins Perama.

The calorifier must be fitted with a pressure release valve at connection C. The overflow hose from this valve can be run to any convenient bilge compartment served by a bilge pump, but the calorifier must be installed so that the valve itself is readily accessible. Most calorifiers are supplied complete with a pre-set pressure release valve, and you should not interfere with the valve settings without consulting the manufacturer.

Connection F is for fitting an immersion heater, which can be run from the mains when you are connected to shore power. This works in exactly the same way as a domestic immersion heater, although you should always use a marine double-protected immersion heater as specified by the manufacturer of the calorifier, which will be fitted with an over-temperature cut-out in addition to the normal thermostat. For example, the Cleghorn Waring immersion heater has a cut-out that, should the thermostat fail, will isolate the heater when the water reaches 90°C (194°F).

FITTING AN EXPANSION TANK

Various sophistications can be made to the basic pressurised water circuit shown in Fig 11.1. One problem that can occur with this arrangement is that warm water sometimes works back from the calorifier into the cold water line, so that water from your cold water taps is no longer completely cold. Remember that the accumulator tank acts as a buffer for the pressure pump, absorbing and storing pressure so that the pump isn't continually cutting in and out in response to small adjustments in demand. An accumulator tank causes water to be delivered smoothly when you open a tap, especially when you only open it slightly, and this helps reduce both power consumption and wear and tear on your pump. However, because the accumulator tank intentionally allows pressure 'give and take' in the system, it can also permit warm water, as it heats and expands in the calorifier, to force its way back into the cold water feed circuit as shown in Fig 11.3.

This problem can be cured by fitting an expansion tank and non-return valve between the cold feed and the calorifier as shown in Fig 11.4, which isolates the cold water circuit from the water being heated in the calorifier. Even if you use a pressure-detecting pump such as a Jabsco 'Sensor-Max', which doesn't need an accumulator for providing a smooth flow, it's still advisable to fit an expansion tank and non-return valve in order to decouple the cold and hot water circuits and keep your cold water cold.

Also, if you don't have an expansion tank fitted, the calorifier relief valve will open almost every time water is heated, causing seepage in the bilge and contributing to a gradual furring up of the valve itself with calcium deposits. This build up of fur around the relief valve will eventually cause the valve to weep, which in turn will cause the pressure pump to keep cutting in and out.

It's important to fit the right size of expansion tank for your particular system, which will depend on the cut-out pressure of your water pump and the capacity of the calorifier. A specialist supplier such as Cleghorn Waring will be able to advise on this, and on the best ways of making the necessary plumbing connections.

You can also use an expansion tank in conjunction with a blender valve to prevent the water delivered from your hot water taps from becoming excessively hot. As with a normal domestic hot water system, the temperature of water available at hot taps shouldn't be allowed to exceed 65°C (149°F) for obvious safety reasons. However, the temperature of the stored water in a calorifier can of course approach that of the very hot water in the engine cooling circuit, which may be running well above 80°C

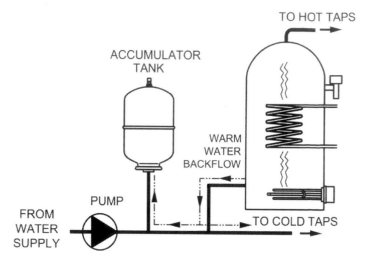

Fig 11.3 Cold water feed circuit showing warm water backflow.

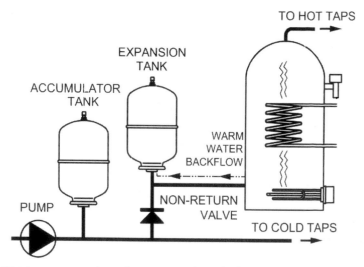

Fig 11.4 A non-return valve and expansion tank can be fitted between the cold feed and the calorifier to isolate the cold water circuit.

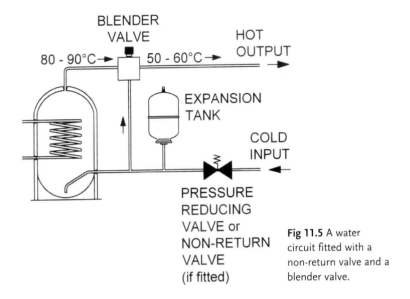

Fig 11.5 A water circuit fitted with a non-return valve and a blender valve.

(176°F). Fig 11.5 shows how an expansion tank can be fitted in conjunction with a non-return valve and a blender valve both to prevent back-warming of the cold water feed and to control the temperature of the water delivered to the hot water taps. As well as providing safe hot water, this system also increases the amount of hot water available.

PLUMBING FOR HOT-WATER SYSTEMS

Plumbing aboard yachts these days is much more straightforward than it once was, thanks to the various modern pipework and connector systems available. Two of the best known are the Hep 2O push-fit flexible piping system supplied by Cleghorn Waring and the 'semi-rigid' Whale System 15 supplied by Munster Simms Engineering (see photograph above). Both systems are suitable for both hot and cold water, and both use push-fit connectors. All piping should be neatly clipped to bulkheads etc using pipe clips, to minimise movement within the system and thus prevent leaks from developing.

For piping between the engine and calorifier, it is best to use heavy-duty flexible rubber heater hose, which will minimise engine vibration transmitted to the calorifier. Flexible hose should be secured on to copper pipe stubs using stainless steel hose clips.

12 | Hot-air heating from the engine

It is strange how, in our cars, we take for granted an efficient hot-air heating system that is always available and that can be adjusted to a fine degree just by turning a couple of knobs. In our boats, however, even a modest size of marine diesel is generating the same amount of potential 'spare' heat as a car engine, and yet there is rarely a facility for blowing hot air into the accommodation while the engine is running. Most owners would find this useful at some stage during the season, even if hot air was simply ducted to a drying locker for oilskins.

For anyone attracted by this notion, it can be reasonably simple to fit a basic hot-air system after a new engine has been installed, so long as the engine has closed-circuit fresh-water cooling that reaches a normal operating temperature of around 80°C (176°F). Various systems are available on the market, but one of the most well made for marine use is the Ardic-Volvo heater, which is distributed in the UK by Krueger Ltd. A schematic diagram of this system at its simplest is shown in Fig 12.1.

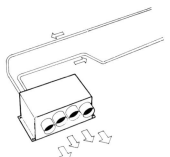

Fig 12.1 The simplest installation of the Ardic hot-air heater.

The main item of equipment is a warm air unit, which is robustly cased in stainless steel, measures 420 mm x 220 mm x 130 mm (16½ in x 8⅔ in x 15¼ in) and weighs about 7 kg (15 lb). This compact unit contains a laminated heat exchanger, through which the engine's fresh cooling water is circulated by the engine's own fresh-water pump.

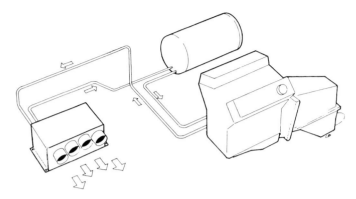

Fig 12.2 Running a calorifier in series with the Ardic hot-air blower.

Air is drawn across the heat exchanger by a three-speed fan, much as it would be in a car heater, and then blown out through four warm-air outlet stubs. These stubs are connected by flexible hose ducting to various outlets around the boat. With an engine water temperature of 80°C (176°F), the warm air blower can generate a maximum heat output of 10 kW, which is a very respectable amount of heat when distributed to strategic points in different cabins. Aboard motorboats or motorsailers, you can lead one of the ducts to a demister at the wheelhouse windows, just as in a car.

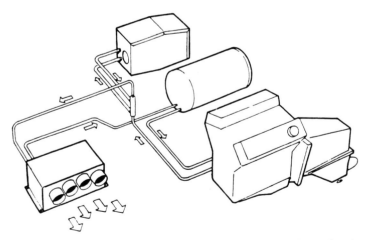

Fig 12.3 The stage-three circuit, which includes a diesel fired water-heater for when the engine is not running.

A further development of this system incorporates a calorifier as well as a warm air unit, so that the engine cooling water is used to provide hot water for the galley as well as warm air for the cabin. This second-stage circuit is shown in Fig 12.2. The Ardic calorifier is heavily insulated in Armaflex, so the stored water stays hot for a long time. A mains immersion heater is also fitted, for when shore power is available.

A yet more sophisticated arrangement, shown in Fig 12.3, uses a diesel-fitted water heater in the circuit as well as the warm air unit and calorifier. When the engine is running, hot fresh cooling water is pumped through the warm air unit and calorifier by the engine's own fresh-water circulation pump, exactly as in the stage-two system. As before, the warm air unit provides warm air cabin heating through the four output ducts, while the calorifier provides a reservoir of hot water for domestic use.

When the engine is not running but is still hot, the cooling water is pumped through the warm air unit and the calorifier by a separate pump, so that all engine heat is used to a maximum. However, when the engine cooling water becomes ineffective, the diesel-fired water heater takes over the heating of the system, providing energy for both the warm air unit and the calorifier. For boats that are used during the winter, warm water from the diesel-fired heater can be circulated through the engine cooling jacket to pre-heat the engine before starting. A warm engine uses much less battery power for starting, involves less mechanical wear, and creates less noxious exhaust fumes in those first few minutes after firing up.

Of course, different boats will have different arrangements for domestic water, and possibly cabin heating, before a new engine is installed. It may therefore be necessary to devise variations on these systems to take account of equipment already fitted. However, even for boats that already have a calorifier hot-water system and full domestic plumbing, an Ardic or equivalent warm air unit is easy to incorporate into the engine's fresh cooling water circuit. It is not just yachts that can benefit from this system either; for workboats or launches with a wheelhouse or cuddy, the advantages of continuous warm air while the engine is running are considerable.

Sadly, more and more debris seems to be floating around in the sea each year, just waiting to jump on to propellers at the most inconvenient moments. Some varieties of seaweed are also pretty devilish, especially for modern hulls where the propeller is not very deep and therefore vulnerable to any kind of flotsam at or just below the surface. While most yachts these days can be manoeuvred with relative ease under sail, we tend to rely on engines more than yachtsmen did even 20 years ago, so the sudden loss of power from something around the prop can be an alarming experience and puts your boat in unexpected danger. Therefore for peace of mind while cruising, more and more boatowners are fitting one of the various designs of rope cutter to their propeller shafts.

◆ THE SPURS CUTTER

The first cutter available in the UK was the Spurs cutter, manufactured in the USA and imported by Harold Hayles Ltd of Yarmouth, Isle of Wight. The Spurs cutter unit fits between the propeller and the cutless bearing, and consists of three main parts: the rotating cutter blades, which bolt on to the shaft just forward of the prop and turn with it; a stationary cutter, mounted on its own shell bearing just forward of the rotating cutters; and a holding block that is fixed to the bearing housing or P-bracket and holds the stationary cutter while the rotating blades chop through the rope or weed rather like a revolving pair of scissors (see Fig 13.1).

To be able to fit a Spurs prop cutter, you need a certain length of exposed shaft between the propeller and the cutless bearing. This length must be sufficient to accommodate the side width of the cutter body, plus a further 5 mm (³⁄₁₆ in) to allow for shaft end play and water flow through the cutless bearing. With some boats, you might have to allow for excessive end play of up to 12 mm (½ in) where no thrust bearing is fitted and the engine's flexible mounts are especially soft. The smallest Spurs unit, suitable for shaft sizes from 18 mm (¾ in) to 31 mm (1¼ in), needs 28 mm (1⅛ in) of clear shaft (which includes the normal extra 4.8 mm (³⁄₁₆ in). Most of this clear shaft should be untapered, as shown in Fig 13.2.

Where there is not quite enough space to fit the cutter, it may be

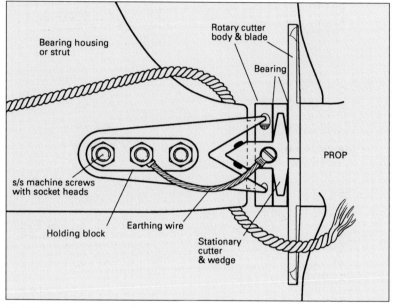

Fig 13.1 The components of a Spurs prop cutter.

possible to saw off a small ring from the end of the stern bearing tube or strut, as shown in Fig 13.3. Other possible solutions are:

- To machine the necessary extra distance off the forward edge of the propeller hub.
- To add a carefully sized spacer inside the boat, between the flanges of the coupling where the prop shaft is attached to the transmission, thereby extending the length of shaft that protrudes from the cutless bearing.
- If the extra distance needed is less than 6 mm (¼ in), ask for the cutter to be slimmed down at the factory.

Sometimes there can be *too much* space between the propeller and the cutless bearing. The Spurs cutter works best if installed immediately forward of the propeller, so too much protruding shaft will mean that the metal wedge on the stationary cutter ring will not reach back to the forks of the holding block mounted on the cutless bearing housing. In this case, you can either shorten the propeller shaft if there is room to accommodate

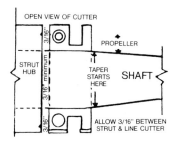

DIAGRAM "A"

**IDEAL INSTALLATION
POSITION**

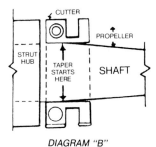

DIAGRAM "B"

**ACCEPTABLE INSTALLATION
POSITION**

DIAGRAM "C"

**IMPOSSIBLE
INSTALLATION**

Diagram "A" shows a straight shaft under an area where cutter is to be mounted. This will assure full clamping of cutter onto shaft.

Diagram "B" shows part of the shaft taper under the cutter. As you can see, this does not give as much surface area of clamping on the shaft, however, it gives more than adequate holding power.

Diagram "C" — Do not attempt this installation. Shaft must be turned down $\frac{1}{8}$" below nominal size where cutter is to be mounted. This removes the taper. We can supply under-size cutters to accommodate your specific needs at no additional cost.

Fig 13.2 Taking account of shaft taper. *Courtesy Harold Hayles Ltd.*

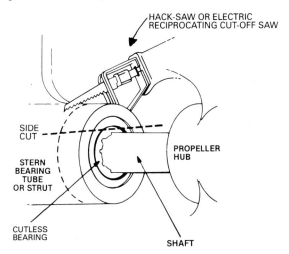

Fig 13.3 Cutting a ring off the bearing housing to make space for a cutter.

Spurs prop cutter. *Courtesy Harold Hayles Ltd.*

the prop further forward, or you can ask for an extension to be welded to
the stationary wedge.

The purpose of this wedge, together with the fork shape of the holding
block, is rather clever in engineering terms. Obviously the holding block,
being firmly attached to the P-bracket or bearing housing, provides the
means for holding the stationary cutter securely while the rotating cutter
attached to the shaft strikes across it. But when a rope is caught between
the stationary cutting blade and the rotating cutting blade, the wedge actually forces the two blades tightly together, overcoming the resistance of the
bearing and instantly cutting the rope. Normally, the stationary and rotating blades never touch, but are held apart by the Teflon shell bearing which
purposely isolates the metal edges from wear.

◆ MOUNTING THE CUTTERS

The rotating and stationary cutters are mounted on the shaft *before* the
holding block is installed. The rotary cutters should first be mounted
immediately forward of the propeller. By way of preparation, the shaft
should be scraped clean and finished off lightly with fine emery tape.
You should then measure the diameter of the shaft with callipers, to

Example of Wrong Cutter Blade Location

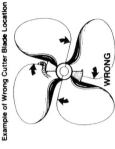

WRONG

When the cutter blade is forward of prop blade the line will lay on top of cutter blade during this revolution of propeller. It will not be cut until next revolution.

DIRECTIONS:

(1) Looking aft, position edge of cutter blade slightly behind leading edge of propeller blade.

(2) Cutter will cut in any position, however it becomes more efficient when positioned correctly.

(3) When positioned correctly, cutter will also be more efficient when reverse cut is made.

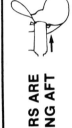

ALL PROPELLERS ARE VIEWED LOOKING AFT

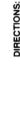
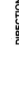

CUTTER OPERATION
The leading edge of the propeller blade draws the line into the cutting blades making positioning of driven cutter blade(*) important.

CUTTER BLADE POSITIONING with reference to the PROPELLER BLADES

Arrows on propeller blades point to leading edge of propeller. **VIEWED LOOKING AFT.**

4 BLADE PROPELLERS

RIGHT   LEFT

Position Cutter Blades Midway Between Propeller Blades

3 BLADE PROPELLERS

RIGHT   LEFT

Position (1) cutter blade approximately ¼" to ½" behind leading edge of propeller blade; the other cutter blade then falls approximately midway between other (2) propeller blades.

2 BLADE PROPELLERS

LEADING EDGE

RIGHT   LEFT

Position Cutters As Shown

Fig 13.4 The correct alignment of the rotating cutter blades. *Courtesy of Harold Hayles Ltd.*

discover where the taper, if any, extends forwards from the propeller hub.

Only up to half the width of the cutter can be mounted over the taper; at least half the width of the cutter must be clamped on to straight shaft. Note that the diameter of the shaft should read 0.05 mm (0.002 in) over the nominal diameter for a good machine fit. The clamping screws are supplied with spring washers, but a spot of Loctite on the threads is a good idea before final assembly.

The position of the rotating cutter blades relative to the propeller blades is important, since the leading edge of the propeller should draw the rope into the cutter at the right angle. For a three-bladed prop, before you tighten the two shaft-mounted castings together, position one of the cutter blades about 6–12 mm (¼–½ in) behind the leading edge of one of the propeller blades, so that the opposite cutter blade lies midway *between* the other two propeller blades (see example in Fig 13.4).

For a two- or four-bladed propeller, position one of the cutter blades approximately 2.5 cm (1 in) behind the leading edge of one of the propeller blades (see examples in Fig 13.4) so that the two cutter blades are effectively in line with the propeller blades (or one pair of propeller blades with a four-blader).

The next stage is to fit the stationary cutter, which is engineered to spin freely in a groove without binding. The cutter becomes 'stationary' once the wedge holding block has been fitted and the wedge located between the forks. Follow the manufacturers' instructions carefully when locating the stationary cutter.

◆ MOUNTING THE WEDGE HOLDING BLOCK

The wedge holding block is secured to the cutless bearing housing with three stainless machine screws, which are provided with the cutter. The right-sized holes therefore have to be drilled in the metal and tapped to receive these screws. You should drill right through the housing and just into the bearing compound, but be careful not to drill into the shaft. Once the first screw hole has been drilled and tapped, the holding block should be held in place as a template for the subsequent screws, to ensure that all three holes are drilled in exactly the right place. As before, smear a spot of Loctite on the screw threads before final assembly.

The wedge holding block should be mounted on the same side of the bearing housing or P-bracket as the hand of rotation of the propeller, ie if the prop is right-handed, the holding block should be mounted on the

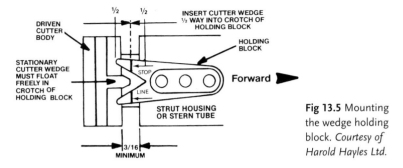

Fig 13.5 Mounting the wedge holding block. *Courtesy of Harold Hayles Ltd.*

starboard side of the strut; if the prop is left-handed, the block is mounted on the *port* side.

The fore-and-aft positioning of the holding block is important, so that the stationary cutter wedge only enters halfway into the forks of the block, as shown in Fig 13.5. This is to allow enough room for any end play of the shaft. Note that if the stationary cutter wedge touches the bottom of the forks during forward end play, this forces the cutter blades to grind metal on metal, as though a piece of rope were permanently being cut, and this will soon cause the blades to be destroyed through excessive wear.

The height of the holding block is also important. There are different sizes of block available for each size of cutter and you should normally select a block that has the nearest height under the optimum height. Then use one of the specially shaped shims to raise the block if necessary, so that the profile of the wedge fits fully between the forks (see Fig 13.6).

◆ PREVENTION OF ELECTROLYSIS

The rotating cutter part of the assembly, being clamped directly to the shaft, can obtain its electrolysis protection from a normal shaft anode, a

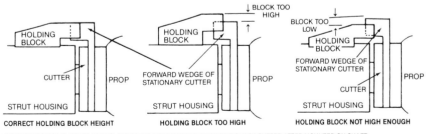

HEIGHT OF HOLDING BLOCK APPROX. EQUAL TO HEIGHT OF WEDGE OF STATIONARY CUTTER AFTER MOUNTED ON SHAFT.

Fig 13.6 Examples of holding block installation. *Courtesy of Harold Hayles Ltd.*

propeller nut anode or, if the shaft is wired across to the engine inside the boat, from the main hull anode(s). However, the stationary cutter assembly must be grounded to prevent electrolysis, either by using the 'flex plate contactor' provided to make a 'brush' connection with the wedge holding block, or by using a bonding wire as shown in Fig 13.1.

◆ THE STRIPPER PROP CUTTER

This British-made prop cutter is supplied by Ambassador Marine of Winchester. The 'scissors' principle of operation is similar to that of the Spurs cutter, but there are one or two engineering differences and all the Stripper components are made from 316 grade stainless steel. There are three rotating blades and one fixed blade, all of which are serrated. The diamond-shaped cutting edges are designed to add a tearing action to the scissors striking action, helping to rip a large rope or thick net into separate, smaller bundles.

◆ CIRCULAR BLADE CUTTERS

A mechanically much simpler design of prop cutter uses a very sharp disc blade mounted just forward of the propeller. Good examples are the Prop Protector by Proprotector Ltd and the Shaft Knife by T. Norris Ltd. This type of cutter is easier and quicker to install than the scissors type although, unlike the Spurs or Stripper, you do have to remove the propeller to be able to slide the cutting disc on to the shaft. As with the scissors cutters, if there is insufficient room between the propeller and the cutless bearing for the rotating disc, you have to fit a suitable spacer inboard, somewhere in the coupling between the gearbox and propeller shaft.

Addresses of manufacturers and suppliers

ENGINE MANUFACTURERS

Beta Marine BD1005: Beta Marine US, P.O. Box 5, Arapahoe, NC 28510. Tel: 252-249-2473 or 800-682-8003, Fax: 252-249-0049, www.betamarinenc.com

Bukh DV24ME: Bukh/Alexander Ryan Marine, P.O. Box 9363, Houston, TX 77261. Tel: 713-923-1671, Fax: 713-923-1972, www.alexandermarine.com, www.bukh.dk

Lister LPW3 or LPWS3: Lister-Petter Americas, 815 E. 56 Highway, Olathe, KS 66061, Tel: 913-764-3512 or 800-888-3512, Fax: 913-764-5493, E-mail: info@lister-petter.com, www.lister-petter.com

Lombardini LDW 1003M and Solé Mini 26: Lombardini Marine/P.R.P., 870 Route 530, Whiting, NJ 08759. Tel: 732-286-6104, Fax: 732-286-4575

Nanni 3.100 HE: NanniDiesel/Waterway Power Center, 2017 Renard Court, Annapolis, MD 21401. Tel: 800-286-8758 or 410-266-0590, Fax: 410-266-0534, E-mail: nannidiesel@waterwaymarine.com, www.waterwaymarine.com

Vetus M 3.09: Vetus den Ouden, Inc., P.O. Box 8712, Baltimore, MD 21240. Tel: 410-712-0740, Fax: 410-712-0985, E-mail: vetus@aol.com, www.vetus.com

Volvo Penta D1-30: Volvo Penta of the Americas, 1300 Volvo Penta Drive, Chesapeake, VA 23320-9860. Tel: 757-436-2800, Fax: 757-436-5150, www.volvopenta.com

Westerbeke 30B: Westerbeke, Myles Standish Industrial Park, 150 John Hancock Road, Taunton, MA 02780-7319. Tel: 508-823-7677, Fax: 508-884-9688, E-mail: help@westerbeke.com, www.westerbeke.com

Yanmar 3YM30: Yanmar Marine, 101 International Parkway, Adairsville, GA 30103. Tel: 770-877-9894, www.yanmarmarine.com

Installing an engine

Vetus den Ouden, Inc., P.O. Box 8712, Baltimore, MD 21240. Tel: 410-712-0740, Fax: 410-712-0985, E-mail: vetus@aol.com, www.vetus.com

Transmissions and sterngear

Sterndrive Engineering, Inc. 1401 N. Myrtle Avenue, Clearwater, FL 33755. Tel: 727-461-0811, E-mail: info@sterndrive.cc, www.sterndrive.cc

Vetus den Ouden, Inc., P.O. Box 8712, Baltimore, MD 21240. Tel: 410-712-0740, Fax: 410-712-0985, E-mail: vetus@aol.com, www.vetus.com

Volvo Penta D1-30: Volvo Penta of the Americas, 1300 Volvo Penta Drive, Chesapeake, VA 23320-9860. Tel: 757-436-2800, Fax: 757-436-5150, www.volvopenta.com

Propellers

Vetus den Ouden, Inc., P.O. Box 8712, Baltimore, MD 21240. Tel: 410-712-0740, Fax: 410-712-0985, E-mail: vetus@aol.com, www.vetus.com

Engine electrics and charging

Adverc BM Ltd USA, Power Premiums, 12557 Dickson Road, Hiwasse, AR 72739. Tel: 479-787-5463, www.advercusa.com

Vetus den Ouden, Inc., P.O. Box 8712, Baltimore, MD 21240. Tel: 410-712-0740, Fax: 410-712-0985, E-mail: vetus@aol.com, www.vetus.com

Controls and instruments

Adverc BM Ltd USA, Power Premiums, 12557 Dickson Road, Hiwasse, AR 72739. Tel: 479-787-5463, www.advercusa.com

Vetus den Ouden, Inc., P.O. Box 8712, Baltimore, MD 21240. Tel: 410-712-0740, Fax: 410-712-0985, E-mail: vetus@aol.com, www.vetus.com

Volvo Penta D1-30: Volvo Penta of the Americas, 1300 Volvo Penta Drive, Chesapeake, VA 23320-9860. Tel: 757-436-2800, Fax: 757-436-5150, www.volvopenta.com

Wagner Products, P.O. Box 221001, St. Louis, MO 63122. Tel: 314-966-4444, Fax: 314-835-1040

Refrigerators

Scott Bader, Inc., 4280 Hudson Drive, Stow, OH 44224. Tel: 330-920-4410, Fax: 330-920-4415, www.scottbader.com

Bilge and deck wash pumps

*Blakes Lavac Taylors: distributed in the US by St. Brendan's Isle, Inc., 411 Walnut Street, Green Cove Springs, FL 32043-3443. Tel: 800-544-2132 or 904-284-1203, Fax: 904-284-4472, E-mail: info@lavac.com, www.lavac.com

Hydraulic power

Lewmar, 351 New Whitfield Street, Guilford, CT 06437. Tel: 203-458-6200, Fax: 203-453-5669, E-mail: info@lewmarusa.com, www.lewmar.com

Vetus den Ouden, Inc., P.O. Box 8712, Baltimore, MD 21240. Tel: 410-712-0740, Fax: 410-712-0985, E-mail: vetus@aol.com, www.vetus.com

Hot water systems

Vetus den Ouden, Inc., P.O. Box 8712, Baltimore, MD 21240. Tel: 410-712-0740, Fax: 410-712-0985, E-mail: vetus@aol.com, www.vetus.com

This is only a partial list. It is not practical to list the multitude of sources for products; addresses and suppliers change and much information can be found in sailing magazines, at local suppliers and on the web. A good source for virtually all marine products in the US is the annual publication *Sailboat Buyers Guide: the complete Guide to Boats and Gear* published by *SAIL* magazine, 98 N. Washington Street, Boston, MA 02114 (www.sailbuyersguide.com).

Index

Other books of related interest:

From John C. Payne, one of the foremost international authorities on marine electrical systems and electronics, comes a new series of easy to understand yet thorough treatments of technical issues facing every boat owner whether sail or power. Each volume is concise, compact, and fully illustrated for easy reference.

UNDERSTANDING BOAT BATTERIES AND BATTERY CHARGING
by John C. Payne

Understanding Boat Batteries and Battery Charging covers the following major topics: Lead acid batteries; AGM batteries; gel batteries; general battery information; battery ratings and selection; safety, installation, and maintenance; charging, alternators, and regulators; and more.

UNDERSTANDING BOAT WIRING
by John C. Payne

Understanding Boat Wiring covers the following major topics: Boat wiring standards; electrical school basics; system voltages; how to plan and install boat wiring; circuit protection and isolation; switchboards and panels; grounding systems; and more.

UNDERSTANDING BOAT DIESEL ENGINES
by John C. Payne

Understanding Boat Diesel Engines covers the following major topics: Basic diesel theory; fuel system maintenance; the function of filters; keeping the engine space cool; how to inspect a water pump impeller; the function of oil lubrication, engine operation and maintenance; electrical troubleshooting checklist; engine instrumentation systems.

SHERIDAN HOUSE
America's Favorite Sailing Books
www.sheridanhouse.com